SOLVING THE PENSION POVERTY TRAP IN 90 DAYS OR LESS

SOLVING THE PENSION POVERTY TRAP IN 90 DAYS OR LESS

ANDREW COPE

Solving The Pension Poverty Trap In 90 Days or Less
Andrew Cope

ISBN 978-0-6455099-5-3

Foreward

This book is dedicated to all who have so far lived a life trapped by convention and peer pressure to live as our parents and grandparents did, to have the expectations of life they had, even though you may now already be in your forties, fifties, or even older. I can assure you that with the advent of today's technology, it is possible to have all your childhood dreams come true in the real world; all it takes is a little dedication and a decision to follow through on the tasks required to step up to the next level, be that what it may for you the reader.

Some say the self-help-Guru-World teaches that you must mend some broken element in your life or your persona. This simply is not so. You already have within you all that you need to be the person you wish to be and to do the things you desire to do.

In this first elementary book, Andrew has illustrated possible steps to take to create a passive income in ninety days or less that could set you on the path to being financially independent. This book is not the definitive or only answer; it is, however, Andrew's hope and a light to give your dreams a new chance to shine and create in you the realization that there is a way you can have the life, the freedom of your dreams and escape the trap that has embraced so many previous generations past.

Fear not; you have found this book, and within Andrew's beloved pages are gems of knowledge to help create a new fire within you and help set you on a path to freedom from the daily grind.

I sincerely hope that you enjoy the book and find it helpful and inspiring. Perhaps it will motivate you to take the first of Andrew's suggested steps – steps you may have been putting off for months, years, or even decades.

Andrew has gone to great lengths to create this amazing content for all readers to enjoy and learn from. He has captioned what he believes you can achieve using his personally used strategies. Read on to see the wealth of information Andrew has to offer.

Pat Mesiti

Dedication

This book is dedicated to all those men and women of mature years whose dreams seem to have slipped through their fingers. With this book and the correct application of the knowledge contained within those dreams can be brought to life.

Never stop dreaming and never give up on those glorious dreams, you deserve to have them in this lifetime.

My Best wishes to you, my fellow traveler on the road to freedom and abundance; remember, you must live as though you are the person you desire to be.

Andrew Cope

Table of Contents

CHAPTER 1

Factors to consider when starting an internet business

When considering starting a personal online business, many people often say:

"How do I start; I can barely use a computer."?

Even though computers have been around for many years now, many people say they can barely use one. What is invariably meant by them is that they cannot do some of the more perceived complicated processes they see the whiz-kids doing. I would have to say, in all honesty, I, too, am in that category; the thing is, though, there is no such thing or person as a computer expert in general, and by that, I mean there is not anybody who knows everything there is to know about every aspect of computers and computing.

Whilst that may be a sweeping statement, once you get chatting with one of these experts, you will quickly find out that they are an expert in one area or another with intense detail, but ask them about another area of computing, and such people will admit they only know a little bit or less. So, my words of inspiration to you are:

1. Do not be afraid of the mouse; it does not bite; in fact, the mouse for many computer users is a thing of the past, especially if using a laptop or a phone.
2. You do not know what you do not know. You might have to re-read that expression a few times over.

3. Adopt the attitude of: Today is a new day. What can I learn today that I did not know yesterday?
4. The beauty of using a computer is you only need to learn what you need to know for any given task.

Before I get into the hardware of computers and what to look for when buying one, let's explore the oldest computer in the world, the Human brain, the thing that makes us do what we do, or so we think.

Because getting your mindset right is the number one step to ensuring you do not give up part way. 50% of businesses fail within three years from start-up, and a further 40% fail within ten years, leaving a potential success rate of only 10% or less. Therefore, knowing what you want to achieve and why is essential before you take the first step in any project.

You are probably beginning to realize now that the key to all of this lies not necessarily in what you think you know or not what you do know but in something much more profound. The secret to success lies within you; knowledge is just a part of the overall recipe for success. It is not even within your heart quite often, and this brings us to a concept that I will discuss with you as we progress through the pages of this book.

Mindset is the key, and I mean that the mind is the combination of the heart and the brain, along with knowledge of any given subject. Let me explain:

I'm sure you have heard the expression 'it wasn't in my mind to do,' 'such and such.'

Or 'my mind wasn't on the job'; let us break these expressions down to understand what is happening within the human psyche.

Until we understand how we tick, we will always be like a ship without a compass at mercy to the events that occur to us all in life. So, what is the mind, and how can we take control to get more of what we want in life and less of what we do not want?

The human brain comprises three physical parts: the reptilian brain, the mammalian brain, and the frontal Lobe; these parts influence our bodies and determine how we act in any given circumstance. Then we have the conscious mind and the subconscious mind; the subconscious mind controls over 80% of our daily body functions, such as breathing, blinking our digestive system, etc.

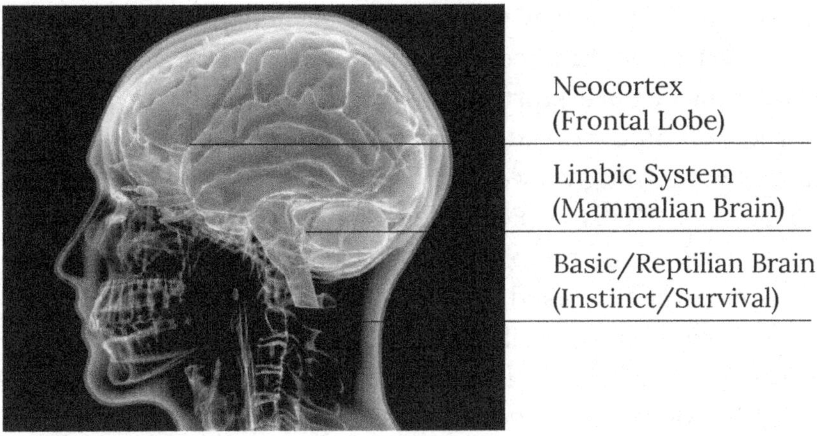

Let me ask you a question. Do you think you are in control of your body, and if not, can our Conscious mind control the Subconscious mind?

Additionally, we also have the Egoic mind, the little voice that says, "I am right, and everyone else is wrong." It gives us thoughts like 'It's my way or the highway' or 'I'm the boss.' The ego can be our worst enemy, but at the same time, we need 'It' to keep us safe.

At least from 'Its' point of view, based on "It's" experiences when we were growing up.

All of this might seem quite deep and unrelated to starting a business and working on a computer. Still, I can assure you that once we understand how we as humans work, we will be able to identify exactly why we act in one circumstance and fail to act when we need to, then we beat ourselves up for not doing something yet once more. Such as New Year's resolutions; how often have you said my New Year's resolution is this or that, only to fail a few weeks or even days later? This is the ego and the serpentine brain are working against you because neither of them likes to change; they want to keep you in the status quo.

I hope you are still with me as we dive into how we can begin to take back some element of control from the subconscious to make headway to achieving the goals and aspirations we desire to have fulfilled in our lives.

OK, now we are starting to create a strategy to reach a desired outcome; consider this point before we continue just wanting something very often is not enough; the desire needs to become a '**MUST** or **ELSE**' scenario.

Our Goals must be extremely specific so that the subconscious becomes focused and believes in them. When a belief is recognized as a possibility, the subconscious mind works harmoniously with your intention to manifest your desire into reality. So, our goals need to be formulated in such a manner as I **MUST** achieve (X) By **TIME** (Y) **OR ELSE** (Z) will happen. Then, we need to record each day you successfully keep your new intention and count the days, but when you miss a day, you must reset the counter to zero.

For example, let us say you want to reduce your weight by 50 pounds. You would write out your goal on white paper with blue ink, and using the formula above, it would read something like I MUST reduce my weight by (2) kilos, so I achieve my desired weight of (***X kilos***) by (***Z month***) date, **OR ELSE** I will not be able to do (A; ***Fit into my new suit***).

Then, you need to make a card about the size of a credit card, write your goal on it, and carry it with you in your purse or wallet. Also, write your goals down as mentioned above using white A4 paper and blue ink and post copies around your home so that you see the goals frequently during the day.

Doing this helps the subconscious mind focus subliminally on your goals. Factors to consider when starting an Internet business.

Remember, we need to keep the subconscious mind working with us, not against us.

Now, consider that you must stop three bad habits that have been holding you back and preventing you from achieving the body shape you desire, such as stopping sugar in your coffee and tea. To ensure that you stick to the new habit, create a diary record and count each day that you have been successful.

In your diary, you will write in blue ink: new habit 1: stop taking sugar. Day (x), write it out each day, and then count the days. Now, if you have a bad day and fall off the wagon, it is OK; expect this: life happens, so try not to beat yourself up too much.

But the downside of falling off the wagon is you must stop the count, reset it to zero, and start again.

No cheating: you are only cheating on yourself if you do. The power of this comes when you have reached 30 or more days without sugar in your tea and coffee. Imagine if you have gone 60 days and you get tempted to put sugar in your drink. Your mind will automatically stop you and say, stop! You have done so well up to this point; do not weaken now; your willpower and strength of intention will help you stay focused on your intent.

Some studies have concluded it takes 66 days, and others say 90 days to remove an undesired habit or create a new one. However, in his book' Rethink,' my good friend Paul O'Mahony says 120 days is optimum to ensure that you completely remove any future cravings.

Now, to add more power to your strategy, for every bad habit that we remove from our new life plan, we replace it with a NEW GOOD habit, such as in the case of stopping processed white sugar in your drinks, using raw Honey instead if your craving for a sweetened drink is strong.

(As a side point, do not be tempted to use sweeteners as they contain Aspartame, and that creates other unwanted issues in the blood-brain chemistry, which is discussed elsewhere in this book)

OK, now that you have a basic understanding of creating goals and we will come back to this topic later. Now, I have an exercise that will help you determine what a real goal is and merely a dream.

But first, please allow me to raise the bar a little higher because, so far, I have only discussed the methodology of creating a goal or desired outcome; now, I want to enlighten you further by adding more dimensions to this process.

We will deal with computers shortly, but we must get our mindset set right first; we must know where we are going in life and why it is so important to us individually.

How old are you, 30, 40, 50, or even older? It has taken you so many years to get you to where you are today, and maybe you are disappointed in how your life has turned out so far. That is ok, because from today, we set a new course, a new pathway to a known destination, and by you following the process I am outlining here, if you do the work, it will give you a clear and precise understanding of where you want to be. Then we can plan how to get you there. I urge you to spend some quality time getting these foundations right and dig deep into your mind to find the answers and the reasons buried within you.

I hope you are ready to start this amazing journey; let us get going.

Firstly, get yourself a thick A4 pad, some pens with blue ink, and some highlighters; once you have these to hand, sit down in an area where you will not be disturbed for a few hours and switch your phone off. I'd say put it in another room, so it doesn't become a distraction, and I recommend you have a drink of water to hand to keep your brain hydrated.

Spend some time now writing down everything you wanted to do but have not yet accomplished. Factors to consider when starting an Internet business. It does not matter how big, wild, or incredible these dreams may appear; the idea is to get everything out of your brain, which you can then review in detail. Do not be afraid to go crazy; nobody else will see your writing.

Making a goal of losing weight as in the previous example, is only one aspect of any given person's life; people have desires, dreams, and ambitions that affect all areas that make up their lives. The core areas of life are Money/Wealth, Physical Health, Mental Health, Spiritual, Social and Community, Family, and Crazy stuff.

Once you have completed the first exercise, please take a fresh page for each area of life: Money/ Wealth, Physical Health, Mental Health, Spiritual, Social and Community, Family, Crazy stuff. Go back to your first list of dreams and ambitions, highlight goals that match each area, and then transpose those dreams onto the new page according to the heading type. So, losing weight would now be on the page of Physical health.

So now you should have seven pages of goals, dreams, and aspirations in each area of your life. Some of these goals may be long-term, shorter, or even achievable in a few weeks. The thing now to do is get five highlighters, each with a different color, and assign a color to a 3-month plan, 12-month plan, 5-year plan, and 10-year plan. Select each dream or aspiration and give it a time when you want to have or experience that dream.

Goal setting

This is a very basic example; I would encourage you to get very explicit in your goals and do a deep dive into the reasons why you want that goal and also a deep dive into the consequences of not achieving that goal. Not just in your head, write the out on clean piece of A4 paper and get very specific:

Money Goals	Why	By When 1 month	By When 6 months	By When 12 months	By When 3 years	Or Else?
I require a passive income A of $200 per month	So that I can create a savings fund	31st of X month in (Y) Year $200.00				I Not be able to do replace any broken items
I require this passive income A to be increased to a minimum of $1000 per Month	So that I can reduce my dependency on having a JOB		31st of X month in (Y) Year $1000.00			I will remain trapped in my job
I require a Second passive income B of $500 per month	So that I can update my car		1st of X month in (Y) Year $500.00			I will Not be able to change my car that may have issues
I require passive income B to be increased to $1000 per Month				1st of X month in (Y) Year $1000.00		I will Not be able to pay for my new car
I require 6 ongoing passive income streams to be generating income in excess of $6000.00/ month.					31st December end of year three Min $6000/ month	If I do not achieve this, I will remain in an employed position and my dreams will be behind schedule.

Remember, once you have completed the money goals, create further sheets for each other live area: Money/ Wealth, Physical Health, Mental Health, Spiritual, Social and Community, Family, and Crazy stuff.

You might find you now have a long list of wants and dreams, which is great, but now we need to start to focus, so pick two or three only from each section of life and set them as a priority of which you want first.

Right now, I would like you to take a new page on your pad and, using a pen with blue ink, write out 25 reasons for each goal you have shortlisted. Do this following the I must by what time or else formula as to why you must achieve your goal; this may take you a little while, but trust me, it is worth it because what you will be doing, in effect, is brain dumping all the hidden agendas within your psyche. It can become quite an emotional experience. Expect this to take you quite a few hours to accomplish, and please do not skip this section as we are starting a dialogue without the subconscious mind, and we need to have our subconscious mind working with us if we are to succeed in our new journey.

Once you have completed that exercise, you will have a clear idea of where you want to go; now, we must map how we got there. We are at the Point where you need to become accountable for your success or failure. Still, we can never fail at anything if we keep moving forward, yes things can side-track us and slow us down and frustrate us even, but with goals written down, we now need to write the steps needed to achieve those goals, and this, for now, brings us to computers.

Using a computer smartphone has become an essential skill for everybody in the last ten years, although I know quite a few people who still use that basic dial-up-only phone. A smartphone is a minicomputer that allows you to run a digital internet business anywhere on the planet if you have power and an internet connection. Gone are the days when you needed an office to go to. Now, you can work from home in the garden or the beach in Bermuda if you so desire.

Before we get into using a computer, let's look at what you need to ensure that the computer you have will do what you need, as there is an overwhelming choice. Although I said you can use a smartphone or a tablet to run your business, and many people do, I suggest using a laptop or desktop with a physical keyboard for ease of use.

A computer is still an important business investment. It requires serious thought, so prospective online business owners should ask themselves a few questions before investing in computer hardware, as the technical needs of online businesses are as varied as those of online businesses.

Here, we have some attributes of computers, and you must have a working understanding before purchasing. If you already have a computer, then it will, if it is a modern one, be more than capable of doing all you need to start up your online business.

It would help if you looked for a few criteria as a minimum specification to ensure that your new computer can complete all the tasks you will be demanding.

A computer, whether a laptop or a desktop, consists of a Central Processing Unit (CPU), a memory system that allows the CPU to move data. This is called Random Access Memory or RAM, a file storage system called the Hard Drive, and not so often now, a Disc Drive to put DVDs in for watching tutorials or making a hard copy of any work you have done. There are also plug-in points designed to suit different and varying types of supplementary equipment, such as HDMI and USB sockets. Then you have the screen where your computer displays what you are doing and a keyboard and a mouse, or finger pad so you can talk to the computer and tell it what to do and for you to input data to write letters and edit documents.

Basic specifications to look for when buying a computer will be discussed; some will be more critical than others depending on your specific requirements:

1. Operating system Windows or Apple
2. The Processor type and speed
3. The amount of RAM
4. Size and type of hard drive
5. Number and type of USB ports
6. Several HDMI Ports
7. Bluetooth and wi-fi connection speeds
8. Ethernet Port
9. Disc Drive
10. Battery duration
11. Screen size
12. Camera quality
13. Sound chipset type
14. Weight and dimensions

No. 1. The operating system

This is a personal preference, much like your phone. Some people like Apple phones, others prefer Android. Generally, Apple products are more expensive to buy, and their software is more expensive should you add additional programs. However, they are less vulnerable to cyber-attacks; some say it is more intuitive. I use both, and I find that computers and tablets that use Windows have more software add-ons readily available that make the tasks involved in editing websites and video content essential.

No. 2. The Processor Type and Speed

The choice of processors is quite large and varied. Processors are measured by the speed at which they can process data (gigahertz). However, to say that the faster the processor, the better the computer is not necessarily the case, as we have seen the introduction of dual Quad and even eight-core processors in recent years. Quad processors can run four separate programs faster than a single processor, even though the quad-core processor may only have a speed of 2.1 Gigahertz compared to a single processor with a speed of 3.5 Gigahertz.

To complicate your choice even further, some dual and quad-core processors operate at 1.3Gigahertz but have a boost on them, allowing the computer to accelerate its speed according to the demand.

Running at a slower speed keeps the processor cooler than a processor continually running at 3.5 Gigahertz, thereby (In theory at least) prolonging the processor's life. As far as individual products go in my experience of building computers, as I used to do, AMD chips are quite robust and serve well. Intel chips, probably more well-known due to TV advertising, are also a good option.

I run a dual-core 8th generation i7 Intel chip on my Dell computer. Budget is an obvious consideration when buying equipment, and it's no different when buying a computer than a TV or a car. The nice thing about Intel's marketing is that you can nowadays (2023) buy an i3 processor powered for US $300 or so, an i5 for US $4-500, and an i7 for $6-900, so it becomes quite easy to see what is within your available budget.

No. 3. The amount of RAM

RAM is a memory chip that communicates directly with the central processor and determines how much data is processed within each computing process. Ram is measured in Megahertz or MEG. The amount of RAM is quite a critical issue, as a computer with 4 MEG of RAM will quickly be seen as a slow computer, especially when it comes to playing, downloading, and uploading Video and when you start working on many documents simultaneously. So, buy a computer with as much

RAM as you can afford; at least 8 MEG of RAM to save your sanity. 16 Meg of RAM will be a great position to be in.

No. 4. Size and Type of Hard Drive

The Hard Drive is where all your data, i.e., photographs, any software you need to create letters, etc., and the computer's operating system files are stored in a dedicated section within the hard drive for safety.

With the advent of the 'Cloud,' many new computers nowadays are specified with small volume Hard Drives, which limit how much data you can store on the computer itself.

Hard drives are sized according to how much data can be stored, and this is expressed in units called Gigabytes or Terabytes. I would recommend at least 500 Gigabytes, a Terabyte even better (1 Terabyte = 1,000,000 Megabytes), or else you may find that you need to buy a supplementary hard drive, which also means you need to have at least two USB ports to allow for the connection of the external hard drive and whatever else you need to connect.

There are two types of hard drives on the market. Standard hard drives are a bit like the old-style record players where a needle scans across the surface of a disc as it reads the data; these can get damaged quite easily in a laptop and cause valuable data to be lost.

Newer laptops have SSD drives (Solid state Drives); this means the drive has no moving parts to damage and is more reliable, mainly when used on laptops. The thing to check, though, is the capacity of the drive 236 Megabytes can fill up quickly if you store films and music videos.

No. 5. Number and type of USB ports

With regards to USB ports, in my view you can never have enough, although I have noticed fewer fitted to the latest computers. Check whether the USB ports are 2.0, 3.0, or less; the bigger the number, the more capacity the port can handle.

No. 6. Number of HDMI Ports

You will probably need at least one HDMI port to allow connection to a second monitor or TV.

No. 7. Bluetooth and wi-fi Connection

Having a Bluetooth connection allows for making wireless connections to your computer for things like your headphones and mobile phone, and a wi-fi connection is needed to connect to the internet; if there is no wi-fi then make sure the computer has an Ethernet connection port.

No. 8. Ethernet connection port

An ethernet port is necessary when the wi-fi connection to the internet is poor or weak; having an Ethernet Port will allow you to connect to the internet Hub directly with an Ethernet cable. This method will also provide a faster and more stable internet connection.

No. 9. Disc Drive

A disc drive is another input to load music and software and create copies of your work separate from the main computer memory. With the advent of Cloud storage, many computer manufacturers are not supplying Disc drives as standard with Laptops. If you need any of those mentioned above, you must buy a standalone disc drive, which you can connect to your laptop using a USB cable. Hence, you may recall that I said earlier that you cannot have enough USB ports as there is always another add-on you need.

No. 10. Battery duration

The larger the battery capacity, the longer the laptop can be used before recharging. Most laptops have a 4 to 6-hour claimed duration, but if you keep the main cable plugged in, you may find that using the laptop in battery-only mode will only last an hour or so. I have yet to find a laptop with a battery that lasts the time they claim in the sales literature.

No. 11. Screen size

This is a question of personal preference, but if you are looking for a lightweight Laptop, you may have to settle for a smaller screen. A larger screen allows for a more transparent information display, making it easier to read and write.

No. 12. Camera and Microphone quality

Sooner or later, you will want to make Videos for Facebook and YouTube so that you will need a good camera and a professional Microphone. Having many USB ports starts to show how useful they are; as you start to do Podcasts and our videos, you will quickly come to realize that quality equipment is essential so that your recordings and presentations stand out from the crowd. The standard Camera, even on the best machines, does not cut it, nor do the microphones, so you will find that you will at some point be buying an add-on camera and microphone to be connected to your computer using a type 2.0 USB port. Perhaps now you can see that if you bought a computer with a small Hard drive, No Disc Drive, and now you need to add a Camera and a Microphone!

So now you already need at least 4 USB ports. And if you prefer to use a Mouse, that is yet another port you need. You can buy splitters, but then you will start to lose the quality of the connection, as you are asking one port to do the job of many.

No. 13. Sound chipset type

Some computers use part of the main CPU for sound processing. Still, more and more are using a separate chip so that the sound quality does not interfere with the central processing work that the CPU is already busy doing. Nvidia Ge force is one of many Chipsets in computer specifications.

As most audio on the internet is uploaded and downloaded in a compressed file format, you will not get the same high-fidelity sound you would expect from a quality music system you may have in your home. Although the sound quality is improving year after year, the point is that we need the sounds we create to be the best quality possible as we are recording so that when we upload them to YouTube or a website, the quality is crisp and clear so that our customers can hear what we have to say quickly.

No. 14. Weight and Dimensions

Weight is usually only a consideration if you travel with your laptop. Generally, laptops weigh about the same as a bag of sugar (2.2 kilograms), although a few very lightweight ones weigh less than a kilogram. However, this weight reduction is accomplished by omitting key elements like high-capacity disc drives and USB Ports. Also, most have small screens. It would help if you thought about all the probable scenarios, you will be using the computer before you purchase the first shiny one that appeals to your eyes.

Now, you have a basic understanding of what to look for when shopping for a new computer; the next is setting the computer up with the essential software you need to run your computer. When you have unpacked your computer, it will come with either Windows or Apple Software already installed, and that software will run through the setup process, which will be straightforward.

But to write letters and process documents, you will need either Microsoft Office or Office 365 more lately Google docs are available, so you will need to decide which you prefer. Once installed, a tutorial will show you how to use that software. You will also find forums on the internet where you can find specific help.

It would help if you were not overwhelmed or intimidated by the steep learning curve you feel you may be on. If you take a step back, you will quickly find that you only need to know enough to get a particular task done. No matter what stage you are at in your journey, you will always find something new to learn how to do.

This is why I spent a bit of time earlier going through mindset.

Most of the time there is a quick fix or easy answer for many of the tasks we face, but be assured I, like many others, who have walked the path that is now ahead of you, find that by asking for help when you need it, from the right person, you will quickly become adept with your new computer skills.

We will deal with computers shortly, but we must get our mindset set right first and know where we are going and why it is so important to us individually.

Consider this: How old are you, 30, 40, 50, or older?

It has taken you that many years to get to where you are today, and maybe you are disappointed in how your life has turned out so far. That is ok, because today, we set a new course, a new pathway to a known destination, and by your following the process I am outlining here, if you do the work, it will give you an obvious and precise understanding of where you want to be.

Then we can plan how to get you there. Please spend some quality time getting these foundations right and dig deep into your mind to find the answers and the reasons buried within you. You are ready to start this fantastic journey; let us get going.

Firstly, get yourself a thick A4 pad, some pens with blue ink, and some highlighters; once you have these to hand, sit down in an area where you will not be disturbed for a few hours and switch your phone off. Put it in another room so it doesn't become a distraction, and I recommend you have a drink of water to hand to keep your brain hydrated.

Spend some time now writing down everything you wanted to do but have yet to accomplish. It does not matter how big, wild, or incredible these dreams may appear; the idea is to get everything out of your brain that you can review in detail.

Do not be afraid to go crazy; nobody else will see your writing.

Making a goal of losing weight, as in the previous example, is only one aspect of any given person's life; people have many aspects to their lives and, as a result, have desires, dreams, and ambitions that affect seven key areas that make up their live experience.

These are Money/Wealth, Physical Health, Mental Health, Spiritual, Social and Community, Family, and Crazy stuff.

Once you have done the first exercise, please take a fresh page for each area of life: Money/ Wealth, Physical Health, Mental Health, Spiritual, Social and Community, Family, and Crazy Stuff.

Now go back to your first list of dreams and ambitions, highlight goals that match each area, and then transpose those dreams onto the new page according to the heading type.

So, losing weight would now be on the page of Physical health. So now you should have seven pages of goals, dreams, and aspirations in each area of your life. Some of these goals may be Factors to consider when starting an internet business. Some may be long-term, some shorter-term, and some may even be achievable in a few weeks. The thing now to do is get five highlighters, each with a different color, and assign a color to a 3-month plan, 12-month plan, 5-year plan, and 10-year plan.

Select each dream or aspiration and give it a time scale as to when you want to experience that dream by highlighting each one with your time scale marker pen.

As you embark on the journey of purchasing and setting up a computer, you might find yourself with an extensive list of wants and dreams. It is time to focus on the essentials. Let us start by picking two or three key aspects from each life section and setting them in a priority you want first.

CHAPTER 2

Using pain to help people find answers to their problems

Now that we have armed ourselves with a few tools, we must learn how to use them to our best and most prosperous advantage.

So, let's begin by asking a few questions:

What is the thing that causes me the most pain, and where do I find the solutions?

Pain is a terrible thing, be it physical or mental pain or anguish; the many types of pain come in all levels of intensity and longevity, from mild stinging one gets from brushing against a nettle to sharp stabbing pain you feel when you get a splinter under your fingernail. These minor pains can be dealt with using pharmaceutical or homeopathic means, depending on where you live and your preference.

Of course, the human body can receive pain in many ways through injury due to accident or misadventure. But other pains can last for years and years, even decades in some cases, like chronic back or nerve pain that very often comes and goes in phases according to whatever strenuous work or activity may have done prior. Still, I will not delve too deeply into those types of pain here.

No, I would like you to dig a little deeper into the previous decisions you made as a younger person, and as we are all aware of the folly of youth, let's not be too judgmental of ourselves.

However, here we are heading towards what should be the 'golden Years' of our lives, and what do 97% of our generation living in the so-called first world come to realize with horror?

We have a pittance of a pension and meager life savings to tide us through the long-anticipated 'Golden years' only to realize when we look at the ledger accounts that those forthcoming years most certainly will not be lined with any form of gold or even silver come to that.

Then, add into the equation that whatever amount you have will be eroded by inflation, time, and unforeseen emergencies that undoubtedly will drain the last vestiges of any hope for a golden year, never mind a few hoped-for decades.

This kind of realization brings about its form of pain, the pain of regret, the pain of realizing as we become more awake everything we learned to do as a child: go to school, study hard, pass exams, and get into higher college or university. You will get a good salaried job.

Looking back, have you found this true for you and your peers?

Just a cursory look at the lives of people who are now in their forties and fifties; what do history and hindsight teach us?

Well, a JOB means just that, 'Just Over Broke' and what is more of all the world's university graduates, less than 5 percent end up in a JOB, (sorry let us be kind), a 'Career' that is in harmony with the subjects they studied at university.

In the UK, for certain, it is quite common to find honors Graduates flipping burgers in MacDonald's with little insight as to how they will change the track that they are on, as vacancies for the type of profession they studied for, quite often are oversubscribed by the time they graduate.

So, they are left overqualified for their current job and underpaid for the skillset they trained for. Clearly, from the get-go, the youngsters of our day and today are in for a tough climb to get to any kind of financial security.

When I was 24, I bought my first house; I paid £12,500 for it back in 1982, and I was earning £5000 per year plus sales commissions selling houses for a national builder.

The average age of a first-time buyer in the UK in 2023 is 34 years old; this is six years older than the average age of a first-time buyer in 2007, which was 28 years old. The average deposit placed by a first-time buyer in 2019 was £46,200. The average first-time buyer mortgage in 2019 was £185,300, with £231,500 being the average price of a home when bought in the UK by a first-time buyer in 2019.

The average deposit for a first-time buyer in London (£110,000) is almost as much as the total mortgage for a buyer in North England (£112,000).

There were 356,000 first-time buyers in 2019, 163,000 more than in 2009. (Source: https://www.finder. com/UK/first-time-buyer-statistics)

Of course, the word Mortgage comes from the late Middle English and Old French, literally 'death pledge,' from mort (Latin Mortuus 'dead') + gage 'pledge.'

By understanding the roots of words, we begin to pull back the veil that has been draped over our eyes for centuries. When one understands a word such as the word 'Mortgage' and how having one or more literally can be a heavy burden to carry in an uncertain job market. This is a factor in so many people losing their homes when they lose their jobs for whatever reason.

Most of us who have reached our mid-fifties will most probably be free from such entanglements, but many probably will not, especially if you have had a divorce in your life, as that, too, is a major pain point. Another factor that escapes many is that for every £100 or $100 that you get in your hand after taxes, it is still taxed further by state taxes, sales taxes, and fuel duty.

The list goes on and on, so that if you were to do an evaluation, you would discover that assuming you have been a non-smoker in your life, you would have paid a further £83+

in taxes, leaving you less than £20 in cash to live on, less again if you indulged in smoking.

So, as we come to the crux of it, is it any wonder that the promised, anticipated golden years you have been looking forward to enjoying are under threat of not being quite golden?

And this is where, if you are brave enough to raise your head from the sand and do the math's, real pain and anguish become apparent because not only may you find that you are in danger of outliving your savings, but there is quite possibly nothing left as a legacy for those whom you will eventually be leaving behind, not to mention funeral expenses.

How do you feel about this as a prospect for your future?

Do you feel anxious, bewildered, let down, or angry?

Perhaps you are pretty stressed out about the whole episode. You may be like many people in our age group, living in denial, realized or not, hoping that things will turn around at the last moment by some miraculous event. But sadly, I can assure you that such a script only prevails in Hollywood movies and not on any of the streets and suburbs of London, Liverpool, Glasgow, New York, San Diego, Sidney, or Brisbane.

Well, now I have picked a few scabs off some old wounds, I am sure you are feeling disgruntled at me for having the audacity to mention such taboo topics.

Well, I am glad you feel that way, and so you should; yes, you should be angry, upset, perhaps even troubled, and bewildered, depending on how deep you feel you are in this hole.

Now, though, let me cast a light, and throw you a ladder so that you can, under your own steam and determination, climb out of this pit and find a new path that will, given a plan and the right compass setting, get you to those golden years with a smile on your face and with confidence in the future you had on the last day that you spent in school.

How can I be so sure about my future?

Because I, too, have been in a deep pit brought about by events beyond my control, and although my journey back to sanity and security has been a long, painful, and tortuous path, it has become my mission to help others who have also experienced similar events in their lives return to equilibrium more quickly and with less pain than I suffered, by not having to navigate their paths by trial and error.

Hence, my writing of this book, which I sincerely hope, will prove to be of some value to you, the reader, in your journey from wherever you happen to be right now to that glorious place you truly aspire to experience in your near future.

So let us begin with an understanding that we all will experience pain in many magnitudes, as pain is a teacher; it tells us something is wrong or out of kilter. So, when we follow this line of reasoning, it becomes apparent that pain is not a bad thing, as when we experience it unpleasant, though it may be, it is nature's way of telling us we need to make changes.

Now, the bigger point is this: How much pain will you endure before you decide to do something about it?

Take being overweight, for example. A cursory look around the local shopping mall will quickly identify the number of overweight community members. Yet, you see them regularly emerging from the cake shop eating pasties and other goodies, and they appear to have no concerns about the effect such foods have on their bodies. Are they in pain?

It would appear not, yet how long will it be before high blood pressure, diabetes, and strokes enter their lives?

From this, as a knowledgeable outsider looking on, we can see people who are on a path to certain harm, and yet, while they may not be in pain right now, they will be in their respective soon-to-be futures, and the damage done may well prove to be impossible to reverse.

We all live to a lesser or greater degree in ignorance about our lives and how and why they are the way they are; even fewer of us have any clear understanding of how to change our circumstances so that we live a much better life with clarity of purpose.

Human beings do not have a user's guide or a service manual.

A fortunate few children will have learned, from their peers and parents from a young age, how to have a balanced, healthy life as they mature. But as I am sure you know; this is not the case for that vast majority in this millennia.

Digging a little deeper into this example, we realize that as individuals, we do not know that which we do not know, and unless someone else points us to some correct and relevant knowledge on this or that subject, we will remain in ignorance and unthinkingly follow the crowd that we associate with, and then wonder how 'I' created such a mess of my life!

When we do eventually arrive at the place of pain, it then becomes a matter of how much pain we will endure before we decide we have no other choice but to take action to correct our lives but until the 'I need to do X or Y' becomes an 'I must absolutely do X or Y' then our respective lives will continue on whatever erroneous path we happen to be on, be it a health, spiritual or wealth issue.

So now, having decided that something must change in our lives to correct the pain we are experiencing, how do we go about finding a way out?

The first step is to sit quietly with a pen with blue ink and plain white paper, and then once settled at the table or desk, breathe six breaths in through the nose and out through the mouth without pausing or holding the breath; don't force the breaths just slow and full, and as you breathe in: say in your mind new energy comes in, and as you breathe out old energy goes out, or you can rephrase to something else such as I'm breathing in positive energy and breathing out stale/negative energy.

Once you have completed that, you need to engage your subconscious mind to get it to work with you and not sabotage your plans for change.

The previous chapter discussed how the mind constantly seeks to keep the status quo. We are about to change that and create a new image of how we want our lives to be.

Now, we begin this journey by writing down the problems that you have in your life and how they are affecting you and your immediate family and friends. Spend about half an hour to an hour digging down into the details of the problems. Once you have done that, stand up, walk around the room, and do some gentle, slow stretches. Add a bit of bending and gentle twists, sit back down at your desk, repeat the six breaths, then close your eyes and imagine what your perfect day would look and feel like if there was more than sufficient money in your bank to pay all the money worries and bills. What would you do, who would you be with, and where would you go?

Now, take a fresh piece of paper and write in detail how you see your perfect day. Spend as much time as you need to do this, as we need to get down to find out what drives you and why.

By doing this exercise we create a vision that we can see where we want to go; it's time to start creating short-term goals, say three months, then six months, twelve months, three years, five years, and ten and fifteen years.

Please do not feel overwhelmed at this point or think goals do not work because they do; you set goals every day but do not realize that you are doing them. We need to take baby steps first and build some inertia; subtly, we must get the subconscious mind onboard, it will help us with our new habits to become second nature to us.

As Einstein said, "You can't solve a problem with the same thinking that created the problem," so we need to change how we think and do things, and then we will see changes in our lives. Hopefully, you are beginning to see that we need to build a new foundation to recreate our lives, or else we will suffer setbacks further along the path.

Yes, I know you want to get to the exciting bits, but please do trust the process, follow along with the plan, and implement each point as we go; you have to trust me on this point, because you will start to feel quite different as your confidence grows.

Now, we need to look at some resources that will help us deal with the pain we are suffering; of course, your pain is different from mine or the next readers, so it is hard to be specific for every case, but the principles remain the same.

So, what type of pain do you have?

There are five medically recognized forms of pain:

- Acute pain.
- Chronic pain.
- Neuropathic pain.
- Nociceptive pain.
- Radicular pain.

We can further investigate our pain by asking ourselves to describe pain in terms of the following characteristics:

- Location
- Radiation
- Mode of onset
- Character
- Temporal pattern
- Exacerbating and Relieving Factors
- Intensity

The types of pain we experience, as described above, would normally result from some specific injury or illness that doctors can readily evaluate. But there is another source of pain that is not quite so readily recognized, which is the emotional pain and anguish we suffer when we do not have enough money to pay the bills or feed our family with the quality of food we would prefer. In these cases, we can point to stress as the root cause 99% of the time.

Additionally, it has been recognized by many Universities and confirmed by the US government that Stress is the root cause of nearly every ailment known to man.

Stress is also created when our subconscious mind conflicts with our conscious mind. As I have said previously, the subconscious mind wants to keep us safe. It will cause us to sabotage any efforts to change things outside the subconscious mind's previous experience or training.

This is one reason your New Year resolutions fail, and you return to the status quo.

Many medical studies have proved exposure to high stress levels over a prolonged period to be the leading cause of all kinds of illnesses, from ulcers to cancer, heart attacks to strokes.

Here is an extract from the US National Library of Medicine:

> **Stress and the immune system**
> [*Our immune system is another area that is susceptible to* Stress.
> *Much of what we know about the relationship between the brain, the nervous system, and the immune response has come out of the field of psychoneuroimmunology* (PNI). PNI *was developed in* 1964 *by* Dr. Robert Ader, *the* Director *of the* Division *of* Behavioral *and* Psychosocial Medicine *at the* University *of* Rochester. Psychoneuroimmunology *is the study of the intricate interaction of consciousness (psycho), brain and central nervous system (neuro), and the body's defense against external infection and aberrant cell division (immunology)* (8). *More specifically, it is devoted to understanding the interactions between the immune, central nervous, and endocrine systems. even though it is a relatively new medical discipline, the philosophical roots of the connection between physical health, the brain, and emotions can be traced to* Aristotle].

The full article link is: *https://www.ncbi.nlm.nih.gov/pmc/articles/PMC3341916/*

Science and Medicine are making meaningful strides in uncovering the interactions going on within human experience and revealing how the life choices we make affect us, maybe not right now, but years further down the line. Perhaps now you are beginning to understand why you are where you are in your life journey. Your childhood lessons cannot show how to resolve these adult issues.

Do not worry or fret; it is not your fault because nobody has been able to explain this information to you; twenty years ago, this information was not readily available, and so today, wherever you are in your life, no matter your age, you can change your path, just by choosing to do so.

Hence, we need to go back to basics, create a new understanding, and re-write synaptic connections in our brains to break free from our current unwanted life, find respite from pain, and experience the life we all dream of having. From this, we begin to glean that the solution to our problems lies within; we need to readjust our internal wiring; how do we do this?

There is no one fixed solution for all but sitting quietly in a room without your phone or other distractions and watching your thoughts, not responding to them, just observing, and letting them go.

I am sure you have heard of the expression 'Monkey Mind,' and you probably have experienced it, or a 'Brain Worm' when you cannot get a song out of your head. These are examples of the subconscious at work running its routines and trying to come to terms with what it has experienced or heard. From this alone, we can deduce that 'You are NOT your thoughts.' What we are doing, whether you realize it yet or not, is your first excursion into the mediation world.

Hence, as you watch these thoughts, picture a white wall where these images, thoughts, and inspiration flashes are displayed. Recognize that none of these thoughts are necessarily good or bad; they are just thoughts without any power to harm.

However, when we attach emotions to those thoughts that is the point at which we create tension within our body and consequently get knotted up inside, our conscious thinking becomes clouded, and that is when we make wrong decisions.

If we can remain disconnected and be an observer only, then we have eliminated emotion and can then evaluate the thought.

As you watch the thoughts, ask yourself internally:

Do I like this or that thought?

Do I want this thought to persist, or should I let it dissolve harmlessly away?

Now, we are beginning to take conscious control of our minds; we decide what we will or will not think. You may find it hard initially to maintain this detached viewpoint and find yourself becoming and owning these thoughts and giving them emotions again.

When this happens, do the six breaths, relax, and then refocus on being the observer.

Remember, your subconscious mind thinks it is in control; we are now surreptitiously retraining it; why do we want to do this? Well, your subconscious mind cannot tell what is real and what is not. Therefore, any new or intense experience or change of direction is treated with fear by the subconscious mind, and it will automatically seek ways to revert to a safe zone; fear creates such an impact on us, but it is also the key to changing our life from where it is today to getting to where we want to be tomorrow.

By creating a conscious image of how we want our lives to be, we implant this ideology into the subconscious, and over time and with every win we achieve, no matter how small, the subconscious comes to realize that this new life is possible, and that is the point when it switches on a new routine, one that works with your conscious derived goals.

It is at this point that we start to see real momentum, and with that, even more belief that you can have that wonderful life after all.

This meditation technique is one of many that can quieten the mind. As a result of a quiet mind, many people report increased health and vitality, as the stressing factors have been removed, albeit temporarily when we are starting, and this is why you must create a set time and place to engage in quietening the mind and do it regularly and make it an everyday routine, early morning and late evenings are best times.

Morning five to ten minutes helps set your mind up for the day's challenges, and the late evening sessions quieten and cleanse the mind from the day's events, leaving you in a more restful mood and giving you better sleep quality. You will find that if you stick to this routine, the benefits will compound over time.

Remember?

The answer lies within us, most of the time.

As we continue in this change, you will notice that you meet new people and new opportunities enter your life, so watch out for such events and create a daily diary so that when you do a weekly and monthly review, you will begin to see progress, and that build up your resolve to continue in this journey. Let us now do a quick review of why we have pain and how we can reduce and even remove it.

1. Mental and Heart anguish types of pain come from emotions, or in another way, whatever we have ascribed a deep emotion to remains unfulfilled and becomes a source of Stress, which blocks the body's energy flow. Which, over time, will lead to illnesses of one sort or another.
2. Physical pain caused by injuries will dissipate as the healing process occurs. The cause of the injury, however, may also leave emotional and mental pain depending upon the event and the person harmed.

By sitting in a quiet room and just allowing your thoughts to pass you by and not ascribing emotions to the thoughts, you then take the position of being an observer of your thoughts; this starts the release of pain by denying the emotions and cleanses the mind and allows energy to flow without hindrance.

The more frequently we practice these easy-to-do meditations, the sooner we will feel the blockages released, creating more creative energy within. We are now learning to control our inner selves, essential to maintaining a new direction in life.

By understanding how we work internally and applying techniques to maintain balance, we can now chart a new course to create a life that we have envisioned within our hearts, with a business mindset that will make us unstoppable.

One of the keys to having a life of joy and bliss is removing the need to exchange time for money to pay our way in this world, so the next chapters will be looking at how to create a passive income using a computer or smartphone and an internet connection

CHAPTER 3

How to create an income without spending hours on your PC

Uncover practical strategies to create an income, all while maintaining a balanced lifestyle away from your computer. These strategies are not only effective but also practical, making it feasible for you to start and run an online business.

Over four point five billion people use the Internet. In 2020, over two billion people purchased goods or services online, and during the same year, e-retail sales surpassed 4.2 trillion U.S. dollars worldwide.

Do you, the reader, now have any reasons to doubt that having an online business is anything but a great idea? The vast potential for success, as evidenced by the billions of people using the Internet and the trillions of dollars in e-retail sales, should inspire confidence in the viability of online business.

Yet how often do we hear friends and colleagues, people we know locally, say buying on the Internet is dangerous; it's full of scammers and dodgy dealers?

Yet, they are the same people who buy groceries online from Walmart or Asda (as it's known in the U.K.) and other companies such as Amazon, eBay, Tesco, or Marks and Spencer without batting an eyelid.

Hopefully, you are on track with me on this point; now, we must wake up and take a balanced view and not allow ourselves to be influenced negatively by ill-informed street talk, which keeps us stuck in our current paradigm.

Creating a profitable online business is different from setting up a car boot store or garage sale, as we must factor in rules and regulations for distance selling. But we will get to them in due course.

To be successful online and because of the myths that permeate, such as the one that 'The Internet is full of scammers, 'we need to use the KLT system.

What is that?

I hear you say. KLT is an acronym for 'Know,' 'Like,' and 'Trust.'

It would help if you considered that for anybody to buy anything from you, they need to feel that they can trust you; this is true even for local shop owners, although we do not stop to overthink about it as we generally go with appearance and gut instincts, these day-to-day tools are not available to use to the same degree when we are looking at a web page.

To help people realize that we are friendly, trustworthy people to do business with, we need to create a bio and a life story that contains your successes, pains, and failures and how you overcame them to be where you are today. Potential customers can now relate to you because revealing personal events makes you vulnerable. They see you are human just like them; it also creates the hero persona, somebody they can turn to for help, guidance, and a possible solution to their immediate problems.

You will see why this is so important a little later.

We place our story on our website, business Facebook page, and advertising campaigns, which we will discuss in more detail later. People can now get to know us, as with any brick-and-mortar business. Such a rapport is essential, especially for distance-based businesses like an Internet business.

We need customers with whom we can communicate and with whom we can reciprocate, so creating a line of communication with our visitors is critical to getting them to like us. We can do this by creating a website or a page on an internet platform that subsequently gives us exposure to the public, specifically to members of the public we would like to have as our customers. More on this in a moment.

Key marketers say that any online advertiser needs to have between seven and fourteen exposures to any potential customer before that customer will act or respond to our messages. You can now comprehend that we are not talking about a here today gone tomorrow type of setup; we need to be considered by our potential customers as a serious business.

We can achieve this using just one specific method or by combining many methods used in conjunction, such techniques as emails we send out on a timed and regular basis, adverts we run, and videos we share, even, believe it or not, old-fashioned direct mail sent in the post.

The more we interact with our chosen type of customer, the more they recognize us as an authority figure; remember the Hero persona?

Then, they are more likely to like us and respond to our messages. How can we create an income without spending hours on our P.C.?

This brings us to 'Trust'. How do we get people to trust us, and what do we say?

We do this by not trying to sell anything in the early stages of communication.

Remember, we are problem solvers, not retail salespersons therefore, we do not need to sell anything to anyone.

Instead, we send them high-quality, relevant, and freely accessible information. Let me explain a little deeper. When a person experiences a problem in their life, they seek professional help, and in the old days, it used to be that they searched the Yellow Pages; perhaps some of you remember them.

Today, however, when people need a solution to a problem, they go to YouTube, Google, or Alexa, which is the same thing if you have yet to realize that.

So, on a day-to-day basis. How do people use the Internet?

Over the last couple of years, people like you and I have used it as a tool. Indeed, since the advent of the Internet, tools like Alexa and Siri have been the main A.I. search engines. People tend to ask. Hey, Alexa, how do I do such and such, or where can I find x or y?

People often use expressions known as key phrases or keywords. The longer the phrase, the more detailed the search. These are known as long-tailed keywords or key phrases. This technology is of great help to us, mainly because there are now other tools that register and log all the keywords searched by every Internet user.

If we use specialist 'add-on' tools like 'Keywords Everywhere,' we can instantly see what people are searching for by the search parameter they have entered in their browsers.

So, instantaneously, we have found a source of pain points in any given niche that we can target with solutions.

Now the question becomes: how do I choose the path most likely to create a substantial income quickly and with few hurdles (fast)?

This is fascinating because it gives us an insight into what sort of problems people are experiencing. Furthermore, with more research, we can list all the common problems of people in each niche or area of interest experience.

Why would we do this?

Because we can now search for solutions to those problems, once we have discovered valid working solutions, we need to package that information into a product so that the person with the problem can readily see our solution as their best remedy.

Or suppose the product already exists in a readily available format and solves the problem. In that case, we can approach the product owner and ask to become an affiliate.

An affiliate is a company representative who gets paid a Commission every time they make a sale. The beauty of being an affiliate marketer is that you have no product of your own, so you don't have to worry about carrying and stocking or dealing with customer inquiries, returns of faulty items, or refunds for products not wanted. Our lives have become very straightforward, and all we need to do as affiliate marketers is connect solutions to people with problems.

Affiliate marketing is by far and above the quickest and easiest way to create an income online. Possibly in a matter of days as you do not need a website, nor do you need to write blogs. Because the creator/vendor of the product we are selling will already provide you with these items, they will give you a link and a piece of code with your affiliate number/link. We copy and paste this link into every broadcast we make so that anyone clicking on that link who subsequently buys the product will generate a commission for you.

What do we do next?

We create an advert in written form that we can send as an email or, better still, create a video Sales Letter. By doing these tasks, we are creating a means of traffic and placing our advert in the forums and places where your targeted customers tend to congregate using this strategy. We can quickly create a list of prospective customers who could buy any number of problem-solving solutions.

But before we dive headlong into Affiliate marketing as a strategy, we must first publish ourselves as an authority figure in that niche. We create a page dedicated to our chosen niche on any of, or better still, all the following platforms: Facebook, Instagram, TikTok, and Linked In.

Once created, we post high-quality, relevant information regularly. The second thing we do is find five other pages promoting products in the same niche; we can register or join that person's page as a member.

Once we are members of that group, we watch and read all the posts; we will see other Members asking questions.

We then research the correct and detailed answer and answer that Member's question. By doing this frequently on each of the five forums, people will begin to recognize us as knowledgeable people and will often seek out our page to learn more about us to see if we are genuine and a person they can trust.

Our Facebook, Instagram, TikTok, Twitter, Clubhouse, and Linked In pages should have links to the products and services we promote, both those we promote as an affiliate and our self-created products or services.

Of course, we would need to create new accounts for each of these platforms. A little tip here is to create a spreadsheet, use a line for each account we open, and record the email address and password we used to join. Also, you will find it helpful to record any Support and Contact Information on the same line if any issues arise with our account.

We can use other accounts, but these are the main ones to focus on to get things moving forward quickly.

Additionally, every page or website we create has its own dedicated link. A great suggestion is to add each of those page links to every other page we create.

To clarify, on our Facebook page, we would place an Icon or image identifying another platform, such as Instagram, Twitter, TikTok, Etc. This means that anyone on our Facebook page can visit our Twitter page or our Instagram page with a single click.

There is a caveat, though: every platform must contain information dedicated to the niche we have chosen. We don't post random photos or posts unrelated to the niche. So, no photos of the family's day out, for example

Using this process, we effectively magnify our presence to the Google Bots that visit our pages sometimes daily, looking for new relevant content so that Google can assess our page rank. To clarify, this means that we have linked every page on each platform to every other page on every other platform. We have become more visible to Google robots, who will soon recognize us as authority figures in our given niche.

Once we have created our foundations, we can create a YouTube channel dedicated to our chosen niche. One of the first things we must do is rank in the top ten on Google and YouTube.

How do we do this quickly?

You can use two methods to get ranked highly on YouTube. The first method is buying an old YouTube account; however, it is a tenuous method and, in some cases, unreliable because the old account may have problems associated with it.

The second and much better method is to create a series of 10 to 15 three-minute videos that are congruent with your chosen niche and do not specifically promote any product.

Can you see how this is the easiest way to create yourself as an authority in your niche?

You don't even need to show your face on camera. Once completed, we will list our 10 to 15 videos on your dedicated niche-related YouTube channel.

Now, a big tip is to load a maximum of three videos per day per channel. If you load more than three per day, the Google robots will also think you are a robot, and the algorithm will create all kinds of blockages against you.

Once we have our 10 to 15 videos on YouTube, we can turn our attention to creating a 20-minute-long video sales letter. [VSL].

A VSL is a specific, well-designed advert that attracts attention to the product you are promoting. You will also need to create a green 'Learn More' or 'Click Here' button, which will have a link embedded within it that redirects the visitor to a page where we can ask for their name and Email address to build our very own list of prospects that we can write to repeatedly.

Our mail software program, which we use to accomplish this, is called an autoresponder; this software will then automatically (once programmed) send out our free digital gift, be that an eBook, a report, or some helpful software.

Once visitors have completed their email and name on the data form, the product page pops up so they can learn more about the product and place their order. The product owner will then pay us a commission.

Once we have a list of visitors, we can start building a relationship with them by sending out regular emails containing free, high-quality information and tips congruent with their niche interests. Another big tip is to refrain from selling them products or services in every email.

Remember, we are building relationships based on Know, Like, and Trust; one way to accelerate this is to invite them to our closed Facebook Group page, where they will receive even more detailed, relevant information.

We do this to specifically create ourselves as an authority figure in their eyes and the 'go-to Person' to solve all their issues and problems within that niche.

Once you have sent out a few emails and created some rapport, you can invite them to look at a product or to a free or paid-in-advance webinar where you will discuss information about your niche for 60 minutes or so.

Our sixty-minute webinar comprises about ten minutes of introduction and an overview of the points we intend to discuss. Allocate about 20 minutes to present the information; for the remaining 20 minutes, we must introduce our 'Stack.'

A Stack is the list of additional related products we give away for Free to boost the perceived value of our main offer. These products and or solutions match or augment our solution to their problem. These products can be things like a list of valuable Assets, Training, and Coaching sessions, each with a cash value ascribed to them to create value in the minds of our audience.

By doing this, we also present a viable solution process that will reduce or eliminate the pain, anxiety, and worry they currently have.

We allocate a price for each item in the stack and then add up all the costs to give a price. We then explain that as they're here today, as an appreciation for their willingness to show up and listen to the very end of the webinar, we will present an exclusive deal, namely a discounted price for people you sign up there and then.

Because we now have a 'warm audience,' our conversions from prospects to clients will be higher than if we had just gone about things in a scattergun type of marketing.

Earnings from webinars can be thousands of dollars from a single webinar, but the secret is to get the groundwork appropriately done first. Once completed, there is no reason why you cannot repeatedly run the recorded version of the webinar to new audiences and create an evergreen product, creating a virtually passive income for as long as you choose to run it.

Now, we can begin to see how to create income fast.

However, I recommend doing a few webinars live before you automate them. Doing this will allow you to fine-tune the presentation and create the best product possible. The benefits are immeasurable. Consider whether you are asleep in bed or globetrotting the world with your laptop. People worldwide can click on a link in your advert, watch the webinar broadcast, and purchase your products there and there.

The business strategy of doing the work once and then getting paid repeatedly for and ever after is a viable working strategy. After all, it has been the same strategy musicians and writers have used worldwide for decades.

If applied diligently, it can and will earn you thousands of dollars or pounds. Once you have completed your research and product package in detail and put together an irresistible offer, there is no reason why that webinar cannot run on autopilot for several years, creating a passive income in perpetuity.

Once you have been through this process for one niche, you can rinse and repeat it for as many other niches as you like. Create another webinar with another product, publish and reap the rewards, and feel proud that you have helped many people solve their problems.

In the process, you will solve yours.

CHAPTER 4

What tools will I need to invest in to get started

Remember that we are starting a business, and as such, any business will require financial input; starting a web business is no different. We will need specific tools to work effectively, so the question becomes what tools we need and what costs are involved.

The first thing that we will need is a title or domain name.

You may have heard of this expression as Internet terminology is now commonplace. We can buy a Domain name from a variety of places, such as GoDaddy and the like; however, GoDaddy, although it charges $8.99 for your initial domain purchase, in the second and subsequent years, you can expect the bill for the renewal of that Domain to increase from anywhere from $15.99 to $25 per year per domain name.

One of the better sources of domain names is a website called 'Name Silo .com'; Name Silo charges $8.99 for registration and each consecutive year after that.

Here is a direct link to Namesilo.com: https://bit.ly/2WoD8RDnamesilo.

Once we have purchased our domain name (we will discuss later how to select the most appropriate Domain name), we need somewhere to 'park' or 'host' it.

Once again, there are a variety of places where you can go to host your Domain. One important thing you need to be aware of when hosting your Domain is that you need to have hosting that is not a 'shared hosting' arrangement.

If you have a 'shared hosting' account and decide to set up websites for clients, when you give the finished product to your clients, they will need access to your hosting account to manage their Domain. Doing that is not a good idea.

You will need to host your Domain on a hosting service provider, and this will cost you money; however, if you sign up to www.Groove.crm, not only do you get all the tools you need to run a successful business, but you also get free hosting both for you and your clients should they need you to build their websites for them.

Groove.cm Sign up here: https://bit.ly/groovesignup4free

When we buy a domain, it is wise not to use the seller of the Domain as the Host provider, as then you could lose control of your business if your Domain name expires for any reason.

We can park our Domain with a different Host to circumvent this pitfall. We accomplish this by using codes called Designated Name Servers (DNS codes), which are given to us by the Hosting Company and inserted in the Domain registration page.

If we do this at the point of purchase, our new website will be open on the Internet within minutes; if we omit this point, it will take a couple of days for our Domain to be propagated.

Once we have set up our hosting account, to create a more professional image on the Web, we must set up a mail server with our Hosting platform so that we do not need to use Hotmail or Gmail accounts.

Now, we will have created a much more professional web presence and appearance, which will add credulity to our business and create confidence in our new clients that we are, in fact, a Bonafide business and not a hobby site.

The second thing we need to do is create email forwarding so that anybody who writes to our new professional email address will see all emails coming in repeated at our regular daily use email address. Which means we can reply without logging in to multiple email accounts. We can respond quickly by seeing emails, enhancing our visitors' confidence in us and our service or product.

Another tool we need in our toolbox is an autoresponder, such as Aweber or Get Response. If you have a Groove.crm account, you get Autoresponders within your package, saving you additional expenses.

All these products offer templates and instructions on how to set up detailed email campaigns, which is essential for us to remain in contact with our prospects and the members of our lists with minimal effort.

Within the autoresponder tool, we park our library of prewritten emails that we send out regularly to our visitors and prospects automatically in response to their initial inquiries or as a follow-up to a sale. Because we send out emails regularly and at regular intervals, we are building further trust and confidence with our clients, and that helps them to know, like, and trust us even more.

We don't need to create a website personally, as many tools are available for building websites. The most common and straightforward route for people creating websites is creating a WordPress site.

The hosting site has a section called 'C panel,' which is in the admin area. From there, we can create and set up a 'WordPress site', which can take a lot of time. However, detailed training on this procedure is also provided within the hosting site so that we can watch and implement it as our schedule permits.

One of the techniques we use to create value for the customer and provide us with an excellent return on investment is a strategy called a funnel.

A Funnel is a method where we progressively take our page visitors from a low-priced product or service to a higher-priced one within the moment they initiate the first purchase without repeatedly asking the customer to re-enter their credit/debit card details.

Two companies are leading the way in creating funnels. The most well-known is Click Funnels. However, there is a newcomer to the block called Groove Funnels. Groove.crm, It is a fully integrated platform encompassing all the tools you need to run an online business in one place; each part is interlinked with Templates and other tools.

Because the software that runs these programs is created by one organization, the whole platform works harmoniously. Unlike in the days past, when you would need a funnel builder, website page, blog page, autoresponder, mail delivery system, and much more, you will now need a software technician to integrate each of these platforms to use them.

All these separate tools will require annual fees currently costing over $25,000 us a year, whereas Groove.crm now costs US$299 per month. Better still, for starting, there is a free version that you can upgrade to a paid version once you start growing.

Groove.cm Sign up here: https://bit.ly/groovesignup4free

Watch a free webinar masterclass on how Groove will set your business up with all the tools you need in one place for free. Go here: https://bit.ly/groovelearnmore

We will need these essential online tools and external tools, such as camera microphone lights and an auto queue device, to help us read our scripts while maintaining eye contact with the camera. We also need a quality computer and a stable Internet connection. This list allows us to get up and running, but we will need other tools to help with content creation.

Other tools and products, such as Canva, Get Stencil and video editing software, will be required to create professional-looking websites and content. We must remember that we cannot be experts in everything; some people are good at techie stuff, others are useless, and they get bewildered, despair, and give up.

Similarly, others cannot put a sentence together and can create beautiful photographic settings. We're saying here to recognize your strengths and outsource your weaknesses.

There are sites such as Upwork.com, Fivrr.com, and others where you can post the required work. People will bid to win the contract to do the work for you, be it building websites, creating content, or any other tasks you need to get yourself published as an authority in your chosen niche.

Once we have created our website and published it on the Internet, complete with content, and are ready to start advertising, we will need to create several Ad Manager accounts, such as Facebook, Google, and YouTube accounts.

Once again, learning how to use these accounts to create the results you seek is an education.

There are plenty of tutorials on each of these platforms to help you establish and promote your products and services. Now that we have the tools and platforms in place, we must seek products we can sell that are relevant to our chosen niche.

You can visit several sites to search for products; the foremost one is Click Bank, which has hundreds of thousands of products at various prices and in every conceivable niche.

Another source is JV Zoo.com and Warrior Plus.com.

Again, these sites are brimming with products that give solutions to people searching for answers in your niche. As an affiliate marketer, once you visit these sites, you will see various details about each product they are promoting; the items that are most interesting to us are the price point and the percentage of commission paid.

Here is a light bulb moment for you: promoting a $29.00 product requires the same amount of energy and effort as promoting a $1000 product; clearly, it makes sense to promote high-ticket-priced products for a commission of at least 50%.

Another element you need to consider is gravity. This tells you how well the product sells in the marketplace, the higher the gravity, the better the product.

An Article Content Writer is another tool or helper you will need to promote your chosen products. You can post a job on

Up Works or Fiverr and have somebody write your article for a fee or have articles prewritten from several article platforms.

Once you have obtained your article, you can reword it and make it your own; that way, people will recognize your style and honesty of writing. To get you fired up in the marketplace and recognized as an authority in your chosen niche, a significant factor in boosting your exposure is to become an author and write a book of about 40,000 words about your niche.

Our article, blog, or book becomes our calling card to be sold for $30 or given away as a freebie or a hook to excite your new audience about what you must share with them. One caveat is that it must be full of perceived high-value valuable content.

It is important to remember that we are in the business of helping people solve their problems, and the more successful we are at that, the more successful our lives will become.

So, to sum up, this chapter shows several items that you need to have in place to start creating revenue; please remember that although this may seem daunting, you only need to complete this process once, and then you will be able to generate income in perpetuity.

Remember your past life?

You were trading time for money. You went to work for forty-five to sixty hours a week for a pay cheque, and then the money ran out before the end of the month.

With this system, you may spend a couple of weeks of hard work but get paid if you promote your service or product.

CHAPTER 5

How to overcome resistance from family and friends

As you read this book and digest the information, you are beginning to realize that you are about to start an epic new journey. One thing life has taught me, and I am sure you are also very much aware of, is that any change is met with internal and external resistance.

Be forewarned; you sometimes feel frustrated and overwhelmed and think that progress needs to happen more quickly. Remember this, write it on a poster and place it where you will see every day as you build a new life structure. Your current life didn't happen overnight, so why do you expect this new structure to come to life instantly?

You are about to embark on a very steep learning curve, and I can tell you many of you won't reach the desired change you have right now.

Yes, that's true; 90% of you will drop out at some point on the journey, mainly because you will think you can save money by going alone.

Let me assure you, very few managed it by themselves, but it cost them thousands of dollars, many dead ends, false starts, and many years of frustration.

Don't believe me?

Read a few autobiographies of the rich and famous; only some have achieved their life goals without significant setbacks and failures. Therefore, you absolutely must get a mentor or coach to hold you accountable for the plans you have set.

Whoever you choose to be your accountability coach cannot be a family member or friend!

Why? Family and friends cannot be relied upon, primarily because they are emotionally interested in keeping you within the bounds of their reality. For instance, if you decide to start a new business, they might discourage you by saying it's too risky or that you should stick to your current job. Or if you want to pursue a career change, they might question your decision and advise against it.

For example, let's say you found a new high-paying position that meant you have to move to another country or perhaps to the other side of the country; family members and friends cannot give you an unbiased opinion to say whether or not you should take the new position because as I said they are emotionally attached to you and have an emotional need to keep you within their circle of influence.

You are about to start a new business, a new venture, a new way of working, or a new way of bringing in income without having to trade time for money; many of these concepts are outside the standard understanding of most people and will be met with ridicule and disbelief by most of the public, even friends and family members.

The fact that you were here reading this book indicates that you want a different mindset to the average person in the street; many people will say, "Ah, the Internet, it is a scam," and yet at the same time, happy filling in their credit details to buy some must-have item from Amazon, E-Bay, or Etsy.

So, we have a point of perspective and an understanding that today, in 2023, hundreds of billions of pounds and dollars' worth of business are being conducted on the Internet year in and year out.

And who is driving this revolution?

The public they are operating as consumers, whereas we will now be operating as Suppliers. Just like these companies...

ebay Uber Etsy

amazon airbnb

What do these companies have in common?

Have you noticed that they don't have any products of their own?

That's right, not a single product.

Did you realize that?

So, what are these companies doing?

They have each created a platform where people with problems can seek out people with solutions and charge a fee for that service. Thus, they are, in effect, acting as affiliates.

Being an affiliate allows you to go and find a hungry crowd of people with a particular set of problems and then provide them with a solution for a commission. By operating similarly to Amazon, Uber, etc., but instead of selling physical products, if you sell a digital or online service, you no longer need big offices or warehouses or guess which products will be the next must-have item.

Furthermore, digital items can be supplied to your customer instantaneously.

One recommendation that I would always give is that this idea that you have germinated in your mind, this master plan that you have for creating your very own independent passive income, is to keep it to yourself and not share it with anyone in your usual circle of influence if you want to avoid ridicule and to become the local focus of laughter, not that any such events are done with malice by your family and friends. Still, they are scared that you will change, and they will lose you.

This is a psychological and well-known understanding of events within the internet marketing industry. Additionally, many people are subconsciously afraid of change. So self-sabotage leads to procrastination and not achieving the ideals they first imagined, so consider how that will rebound when you don't immediately achieve what you postulated to your family and friends! Your first battle is with your subconscious mind; it will do anything and everything, as mentioned previously, to retain the status quo. It never ceases to amaze me how often other events arise when you are trying to concentrate on your new venture.

The universe will test your resolve to see how determined and how much belief you have in yourself that you will attain and achieve the dreams you have set before yourself. It would help if you created new habits that keep you focused and on track, and for every new habit, you need to remove an old, unproductive habit.

One little trick to keep you focused and to maintain yours is to record in a diary how many days you are undertaking your new habit and removing your old habit once you get to, say, 300 days of not having sugar in your coffee, for example, the pressure not to have that spoonful of sugar in that cup of coffee is immense because you know that if you do succumb and take that spoonful of sugar on your 301st day, then you have to start all over again from zero.

This is the way to keep count of your progress and maintain inertia (forward momentum).

Your second battlefront is with family and friends. My heart recommends that you tell them as little as possible until you have results. Then, they will ask you where you got that BMW from and how you managed it.

Indeed, let the results speak for you, and then all the antagonistic banter from the naysayers will be silenced. Do not underestimate the effects of antagonistic banter and ridicule on your psyche; as mentioned earlier, people do not like change even when that change brings a brighter future.

Also, remember that you are on an intense learning curve, and you may need the answers to their comments, which can undermine your confidence in yourself and your progress.

While this is only a short chapter, the enormity of the repercussions if you succumb to negative influences will affect your entire future and those around you. We will learn, however, and we will dive much deeper into managing our mindset to ensure success.

Remember when we spoke earlier about how important it is to write out your goals 100 times and to write them in a negative context? By that, I mean your goals must be as follows: I must achieve X by time Y, or Z will be the consequence.

For example, I must earn an extra US$1000 a month by May 31st, 2024, or else I won't be able to buy the latest iPhone at its launch.

Remember, once you have completed the money goals, create further sheets for each of the other living areas: money, Wealth, Physical Health, Mental Health, Spiritual, Social and Community, Family, and Crazy stuff.

You must remain firm in your resolve to maintain this path in creating a passive income that will allow you to make the choices that truly matter in your life by spending time with whom you want, whenever you want, as often as you want.

This, then, is our destination, but make no mistake, there is a lot of hard work and also a steep learning curve to overcome, but the rewards will be well worth all the effort you are about to invest; you will be able not only to create a passive income and more but also there exists a genuine possibility that you will create a legacy for those to benefit from when you're no longer here.

Clear your mind, write out your goals, set your resolve, learn to keep quiet about your intentions to those in your immediate circle, and create new contacts and friends walking the same path you have now begun to walk.

I mentioned earlier that if you mix with people who have ideas worth £100, you will also have ideas worth 100 pounds; if you mix with people whose ideas extend to 1000 pounds likewise so your ideas will extend to 1000 pounds; what about if you are mixing with people whose ideas cost £1,000,000 will not your ideas also be in that same million-pound bracket.

Einstein said you cannot resolve a problem with the same mindset that created it. From the beginning, I have said we must change our minds to change our destiny.

I trust that you, too, are now of the same mindset, and I look forward to walking this path with you to a better and more prosperous future. In the next chapter, we will discuss creating a robust business mindset that will make you unstoppable in any area of life.

CHAPTER 6

Six Steps to Overcome Failure and Keep Growing

Failure is an inevitable part of life; it can be challenging to bounce back from a setback. Procrastination and fearful thoughts like 'I'm not good enough' or 'I can't do this.' However, with the right mindset and strategies, overcoming failure and growing as an individual is possible. Having your goals and strategy written down in written form is an invaluable asset that keeps your mind focused on the end game. This chapter will explore some practical tips and techniques for overcoming failure and continuing to grow.

1. Embrace Failure

One of the first steps in overcoming failure is to embrace it as a natural part of the process. Rather than viewing failure as a negative outcome, try to see it as an opportunity for growth and learning. When you fail, you can reflect on what went wrong and adjust your future actions to avoid similar mistakes.

Einstein said, "We cannot solve our problems with the same thinking we used when we created them. "Additionally, accepting failure can help reduce the stress and anxiety that often accompanies setbacks, allowing you to approach the situation more clearly. Remember also, when dealing with a market, we often learn that what you and I think is good is different from what the masses in the niche we are working with think is good. Let the market guide us to what they want that solves their problems.

2. Learn from Failure

Once you have embraced failure, taking the time to learn from it is essential. Analyze what went wrong and identify any patterns or underlying issues contributing to the loss. Ask yourself what you could have done differently and what you can do in the future to avoid similar situations. Taking this time to learn from your failures can increase your chances of success and minimize the likelihood of making the same mistakes.

3. Seek Support

Overcoming failure can be difficult, and it is essential to have a support system in place. Whether it is friends, family, or a mentor, having someone to talk to and share your experiences with can help you stay motivated and on track. Additionally, seeking support could help you gain new perspectives and insights into your situation, which can be invaluable in overcoming failure and growing as an individual.

It is best to seek support from someone you know who has already succeeded in your path, as such people can give you the right advice as they already have the mindset you are developing. If you seek support from someone who isn't on your wavelength, you will get the wrong advice, which may lead to you giving up on your desired reality just so that you fit in with the circle of friends you have been with. Remember, you are seeking to change your reality, and that process will lead to you gaining new friends and acquaintances, but it will also mean old friends can no longer relate to the frequency at which your body will now be vibrating, so you will find that you see these people less and less. It's a natural process and only to be expected.

4. Stay Positive

One of the keys to overcoming failure is to maintain a positive attitude. While it can be tempting to focus on the negative aspects of a setback, it is essential to remember that lapses are momentary, and that success is often just around the corner. By staying positive, you can increase your prospects of success and maintain a healthy outlook on life.

A positive outlook can help reduce stress and anxiety, allowing you to approach these challenges. A keyway to stay positive is to reflect on your desired outcome every morning when you wake up and every evening when you are about to sleep. If you do this religiously, then after 28 days or so, you will find that your subconscious mind will begin to deliver new circumstances, and you will experience events in your life that will push you to your desired outcome in leaps and bounds.

5. Stay Focused on Your Goals

It is also essential to stay focused on your goals and continue to work towards them, even after a failure. Remember that setbacks are temporary and a necessary learning curve. Remember you are on a journey, not a 100-meter dash, and that success is possible with the right mindset and approach. Remain focused on your goals and continue to work towards them, implementing the lessons learned from your failures to hone your skills. Remember, when undertaking new tasks, do a test run first to keep costs down.

Once you verify some small, consistent success, you can scale and invest more assets into the scheme only when the campaign delivers repeatable, proven results. At the other end of the process, you will find that, as in the case of an advert, the process will peak, level, and then tail off. So constant monitoring and fine-tuning are essential to save wasting assets on the tail end.

6. Keep Moving Forward

Finally, it is essential to keep moving forward and not let failure hold you back. While it can be challenging to bounce back from a setback, it is crucial to stay motivated and focused on your goals, take the time to reflect on your experiences, keep a diary on your success so far, look back at how far you had come from when you first started this venture. Learn from your failures and use that knowledge to temper your actions.

By maintaining a forward-moving momentum, you can overcome disappointment and continue to grow as an individual. Methods that millionaires use to overcome setbacks of all kinds. I want to set in your mind the thoughts and feel the emotions you would have as though you are already a millionaire.

Remember, the subconscious mind cannot tell the difference between imagination and reality because the language the subconscious understands is the language of emotions. So, if you are dwelling in the emotion of doubt and fear, guess what?

That's the vibration your body sends out to the universe, and the universe responds by sending you more events that create even more doubt and fear within you. The universe is impartial, it will give you whatever you ask for immediately in the cosmic realm, but to manifest it here in the 3D earth realm, you absolutely must be on the matching vibrational frequency of the thing or experience you are desiring and beholding that frequency until you have it in your possession.

Any let-up in your vibration will cause delays in your receiving the desired thing or event. Now consider the criteria your mind must have to successfully navigate the birth of a new project to its completion. During this journey, as we have already discussed, failure and setbacks will be events you will experience that may create bigger obstacles on the path to success. You must not succumb to the emotions these events bring, as that will send your vibration off the frequency you need to complete the manifesting process.

Still, thinking with a millionaire mindset is the key to overcoming those trip hazards and avoiding the stress they can induce, which means getting control of your emotions. Especially emotions of anger, frustration, and doubt. Instead, cultivate gratitude and love for those around you, even when the same people let you down knowingly or unknowingly.

As we know, millionaires already play with a stacked deck before doing anything, so let's look at some of the tools they already have. We will consider seven elements they have put in place before starting a new venture; likewise, if you put these in place, they will significantly enhance your success rate.

1. Millionaires have a mental toughness:
   They often have a strong mental attitude that allows them to overcome adversity in all its forms. They must maintain a positive outlook, be resilient, and have a growth mindset no matter what life throws at them. Reflect on this in yourself. How does your mindset measure up to this standard?

2. Planning and Preparation:
   Millionaires are known for having a clear plan in place, which helps them navigate through tough times by having 'Contingency Elements and 'What If' elements. Also, it includes having a well-drafted financial plan and regular reviews to track progress. If you still need to write your strategy out, note these details and sub-categories so you have them put in place at the outset.

3. Networking:
   Millionaires are well known for understanding the importance of having a solid network of people who can support them during difficult times. Including having mentors, forming alliances with other millionaires, and seeking advice from trusted professional advisers.

4. Adaptability: millionaires have quick-thinking minds that allow them to adapt to changes in the marketplace and their personal lives on the roll of the dice. Life throws curve balls at us all the time, and we need to be quick on our feet to react when they come our way. By being open to new ideas, embracing new technology, continuously learning and growing, and implementing these new skills and knowledge within their business, they are always at the forefront in the marketplace in which they operate.

5. Financial Management:
   Millionaires understand the importance of financial literacy and have a strong understanding of money management. Having a realistic budget, reducing debt, and investing in assets that generate additional income on a passive and active methodology.

   They also understand the concept of OPM, 'Other People's Money.' What does this mean? Other people's money (OPM) is a strategy that allows a businessperson to invest in a business project by using other people's money, thereby not putting his own assets at risk.

   Crowdfunding, using a bank, using an insurance contract, taking on other business partners, or selling a given product before its creation are all methods of spreading risk.

   These powerful techniques test the viability of your product within the marketplace that you are targeting with reduced risk to your asset base. People will only buy a product after its creation, or so you would think. Still, they will buy into a concept that gives them a clear understanding of an outcome that will solve an issue or a problem that a particular group of people requires a solution to.

6. Focus:
   Millionaires can maintain focus and discipline, even during tough times. They stay focused on goals, avoid distractions, and manage time effectively. Millionaires and executives very often lock themselves within their office and business community until the project is successful. Writers, authors, and copywriters also can spend hours, even days, just brain-hacking ideas before committing to a given path or course. You must ask yourself, is this something you can do yourself? Is this something that your current relationships would tolerate?

   If you have any doubts, you need to enter meaningful conversations with your significant other so that they understand what it is you intend to achieve and that they, in time, will also benefit from your diligence and success.

7. Gratitude:
   Millionaires understand the importance of being grateful for what they have, even during difficult times, by expressing gratitude for their relationships, their health, and the opportunities that come their way. Gratitude is the highest vibrational frequency that a human can emit. You may have heard of the law of attraction; I did touch on that subject earlier. Still, only a few understand it is a secondary law governed by its primary law, the law of vibration. So many people trying to use the law of attraction to change their lives have yet to see tangible results for all the effort.

   Because their body's vibrational frequency does not align with what they wish to attract, frustration and feelings of lack and poor worth can set in, thereby further sabotaging their efforts!

How do we know what our vibrational frequency is?

We need to focus on how we feel in our hearts because when we focus on our hearts, we ask ourselves what our current emotions are:

Am I feeling happy, sad, frustrated, joyful, or loved?

Each of these emotions causes your heart to vibrate at a given frequency, and the law of attraction sends more of this frequency back to you from the cosmos. The essence of 'The rich get richer; the poor get poorer.'

How would you feel if you had a million in the bank? How about ten million?

Would having such an asset base open fewer door of opportunity for you to expand and grow more?

Gratitude is the highest frequency of vibration; if we can maintain this high frequency, over time, our lives will change; they must change because it is the law of like attracts like, aka the law of attraction.

By maintaining this high frequency, we will continually attract more opportunities, events, and circumstances that allow us to meet other people who are also vibrating at that frequency. New friendships and alliances can create new opportunities for growth and unexpected changes for the better. Often our lives can change dramatically overnight.

Please write down ten things you are grateful for in each area of your life. Love, money, health, spirituality, intellect, and family can be challenging, especially if you feel down and life is tough.

But do this at whatever level you can and read them daily, carry them with you daily, review them, and add to them as new things occur. You might lose your home, job, or lover, and your heart may be tattered.

However, if you are still breathing, there is still time, and a little down the road, there will be a better home, a more loving lover, and a higher-paying job. But the longer you remain in a low vibration, the longer it will take to be in that better place, expressing gratitude and love for your fellow man, especially the ones that have done you wrong. Joy and peace, I promise you your life will change for the better.

I would also encourage you to keep a diary and keep a note in that diary of your emotions during the day, you see we can start the day feeling joyous and happy, get into our car, and within 15 minutes of driving, be feeling angry and frustrated because of other drivers or road conditions.

How will you attract anything you desire while vibrating at such low frequencies?

Can you now see how important it is to know what is happening in our minds?

It is crucial that when we experience a change of emotions and feelings during the day, we immediately think of something of a higher vibrational value. The more you do this, the more intuitive it will become. That way, we can maintain an overall higher vibrational frequency and attract more of what we want and less of what we don't want.

In conclusion, overcoming failure is integral to growth and development, embracing failure, learning from it, seeking support, staying positive, staying focused on your goals, and moving forward. I can't emphasize the importance of keeping the momentum going, no matter how small.

Remember, millionaires fail 80% of the time, so just like them, you can overcome setbacks and continue to grow as an individual.

Whether working towards a personal or professional goal, remember that failure is just a temporary setback, and that success is possible with an ongoing right mindset and a determined thought-out approach.

CHAPTER 7

Creating a business mindset will make you unstoppable

Creating a business mindset will make you unstoppable

Before buying a domain name, we need to set out our plan.

Before we even do that, we must reset our minds and thinking.

We will investigate some of the laws of success presented in my course because every entrepreneur needs to understand some basic but little-appreciated facts before embarking on any business project; get this wrong by needing to fully understand some of the laws and disasters lurks around the corner.

You must understand that being an entrepreneur is not just about the money; everybody needs a helping hand, so we are going to explore a few of the laws governing the success of every entrepreneur as found in my '30 days to change your mind, change your life' business coaching program, a course in helping you manifest a new and empowered life.

While studying these laws each day, we will subtly change how we think and, in that process, bring the subconscious mind on track to working with us and not against us.

I recommend that you study one law daily, apply it, think about it during the day, and consider how you can implement it in your life.

Make notes in your daily journal as realizations spring to life within your mind. Suppose you undertake to commit to doing this diligently. In that case, you will reprogram the way your mind works by breaking synapse connections that no longer serve you and creating new synapses that will strengthen your resolve to be the person you dream of becoming, and that in turn will set, you up for the success you richly deserve.

Ok, so here are the first laws.

Day One — Law One:

Which picture do you relate to the most?

Picture 1:

Picture 2:

Become the person you envisage in your dreams

Let's begin by considering our most dominant images of ourselves.

When you look at yourself in the mirror, what do you see?

What image of you dominates your life?

What image of your business dominates your life?

Whatever that image is, it is that to which you will gravitate towards.

You cannot have two competing thoughts simultaneously; one will always dominate.

The Christian bible says, "No one can serve two masters, for either he will hate the one and love the other: or else he will be devoted to one and despise the other." Mathew 6:24). It is the same within your mind.

If your mentality is one of lack, if you have an "I am not worthy" mindset, if you are doubleminded ("Yep, like to be prosperous, but I don't believe I can put the effort, energy and focus into my life to attain the prosperity I desire"), then you will never be prosperous.

You have two competing thoughts, creating split energy.

On the one hand, you desire prosperity, but on the other hand, your mindset is one of lack – not enough, not good enough, not doing enough. This mindset dominates your self-image, and with that mindset, do you honestly believe you will reach your goals?

Day Two — Law Two:

Which picture do you relate to the most?

Picture 1:

Picture 2:

Bury your past: Your future lies beyond the mist

These are two kinds of memories in life – good and bad- and both kinds of memory ruin prosperity.

I love this quote from Walt Disney:

> *"I don't like to repeat success;*
> *I like to go on to bigger and better things."*

What a brilliant statement!

Bad memories are like chains around our ankles that hinder us from moving forward. Good memories can become hammocks in which we rest.

Here is some great news – no one has a functional past. We are all, in one way or another, victims of dysfunction.

Mistakes, hurts, fears, and failures should be the springboard to your future success. You will learn more from the tragedies of your past than you will ever learn through the good times.

You must get over your past, be more significant than your past, and not dwell on your disappointment about those past events.

Your prosperity quotient must be more significant than your disappointment quotient. Many people get stuck in the past because they continually look in their life's rear vision mirror.

You cannot go forward while you are constantly looking backward.

It's like the elephant at the circus. This colossal beast is held captive by a small rope and a little stake in the ground.

How?

> When the elephant was a baby with very little strength, it tied a strong rope around its ankle attached to a stake in the ground to keep it from roaming. Because of its good memory, the elephant never forgets that the stake and the rope prevent it from moving away. Therefore, the elephant remains a prisoner of its past, even though it could easily break free.

Because when the elephant was a baby with very little strength, it tied a strong rope around its ankle attached to a stake in the ground to keep it from roaming. Because of its good memory, the elephant never forgets that the stake and the rope prevent it from moving away and therefore the elephant remains a prisoner of its past, even though it could easily break free.

Now, you must ask yourself .... What is your stake in the ground?

What is hidden in your past holding you captive to your current paradigm?

We must learn from our past, not complain about and bemoan our previous plight.

Adversity reveals two things:

1) Who we are and what we are made of.

2) What we believe.

I'm sure most of you reading this book have driven or even walked down a country lane in the dead of night; how far can you see?

Without a torch or car headlights, it is not very far; on a moonless night, you probably can't even see your hand in front of your face.

So how does a driver maintain a safe path down a country lane in the dead of night?

The driver drives at a speed they can see within the distance of the headlight beams. And this analogy is accurate to life, too. We can never know what the next moment will bring, but if we follow a plan of action based on known probabilities, we can navigate life.

Likewise, when starting a new venture, we need to gather all the information we can to set a course of action; a step-by-step approach will keep us safely on the path to success, assuming that each step has been verified.

This is a crucial reason why the most successful people follow the paths of those who have already completed the route we are endeavoring to follow.

Day Three — Law Three:

Which picture do you relate to the most?

Picture 1:

Picture 2:

Whatever you tolerate you will never change

"I hate being broke," ...
"I don't like my Staff being late," ...
"I'm sick of being overweight," ...
"I hate being unhealthy," ...
"I don't like my bad temper," ...
"I don't like my bad spending habits" ...

How often do we find ourselves saying things like these?

The hard truth is you like those things.

Otherwise, you would stop doing them in an instant.

Before you object, let me reason with you why I think this – If you don't like a thing or a situation, you won't tolerate it, would you?

Think of a food you hate; Consider that food served in a restaurant. Would you eat it?

Chances are you wouldn't because you may well be physically sick by doing so.

However, the other things mentioned at the start of this section do not necessarily affect you with such a dramatic effect that you are consciously aware of, so you allow them to remain in your current reality.

Let me give you a simple illustration of what I mean. Somebody may say, "I don't like beetroot. I hate beetroot with a passion!" They may even say, "I think an eternal punishment would be eating beetroot every day for the rest of your life."

You may even say: I hate beetroot so much I will not tolerate it. Not with a hamburger nor in a salad. I refuse to have it because I won't tolerate it. Full Stop.

If a smoker says to me, "I hate smoking," my reply is, "Then why do you smoke?"

If you hated it, you wouldn't tolerate it – you wouldn't smoke, but as it has become a habit in your current reality, you continue to be subject to the cravings.

What is a habit?

A habit is a subconscious program you instill into your subconscious mind, and now you no longer think about it; you do that habitual action unconsciously.

Likewise, we can expand this thought process to...

Do you hate being stuck at your income level right now?

Are you disappointed with the amount of lack in your life?

Are you tolerating a small business mindset?

If you are, it is time to stop it!

When we tolerate, then we navigate and make excuses.

What do I mean by this?

When we tolerate things in our lives, we tend to navigate around those things, making excuses for being the way we are.

If you don't tolerate a thing or circumstance, you won't navigate. Instead, you will instigate new habits, new behaviors, and new ways of thinking in your life to remove or get free from the circumstance or thing that you can no longer tolerate.

The reason to change anything must grow from a WISH to a NEED to an absolute MUST before your subconscious mind will allow you to effect the changes necessary to escape.

Remember, you cannot change something you or your subconscious mind consistently tolerates. IT .... The subconscious mind runs your life 90% of the time by running patterns or programs we have allowed in during the first 30 years of our life.

We are prisoners to those programs until we identify the ones that no longer serve us and actively work on programming them out by replacing them with new programs that serve us.

Day Four — Law Four:

Which picture do you relate to the most?

Picture 1:

Picture 2:

It would help if you allowed money to flow like a stream, not become a stagnant pool.

Money makes the world go round. Does it?

How many of you think that money is always in short supply?

or that experience the "Too many days in the month before payday comes around again" feeling?

How often did your parents say to you? "Money doesn't grow on trees. "or "Money's too tight to mention"?

Many people have the 'Pie' mentality about all sorts of commodities, especially money; they think that if someone else has a lot of money, then there is less for them to have.

Is this the way you think?

Let me ask you another question ... What happens to the money stored under the bed?

In the UK, many years ago, people used to store white five-pound notes under the bed in case of a rainy day. But what happened?

The UK Government issued a new banknote so that the old white fivers became worthless overnight!!

Many of the people who stored the money tried to exchange the old white five-pound notes for the new notes, which raised issues for them with the Tax office, which in turn created further problems.

So, one could liken this episode to a thought that money can be stored, but as we can see, any pool of water that doesn't flow becomes stagnant.

Likewise, we must make our stored money work and flow to create new money to maintain its value.

Some say money is a tool or oil to smooth a person's way through life; this may be true to some degree.

However, a more accurate description of money would be that it is a "Measure of how much someone else is willing to pay you for your service or product."

Before we move on, we also need to consider inflation and its effect on people, especially now in the autumn of 2023, as many families around the world are worried about rising costs of fuel for their cars and heating their homes, the cost of food is spiraling out of control.

Wages do not match these costs, so poverty is quickly becoming a fact for many people who once thought of themselves as comfortable with the cost of living.

More of a sinister fact is that this process orchestrated by those who control the systems that further programs the minds of the people into a poverty state of mind.

Thus, limiting their innate ability to change their current reality to one of abundant life. We all have this ability to change our day-to-day reality, and we can do it by changing our perspective of ourselves.

For many people, money issues and ideas about how the world works have been formulated by their parents and even their grandparents, parents, so ingrained is our mental conditioning.

If, though we consider money in another light, magical things can happen in our lives, consider with me some alternative views on money.

Whether we have considered it or not, we all live in an abundant universe, and you don't ever doubt that there is enough air or water to drink.

Do you?

Even in the driest climates, water still needs to be found, but you need accurate knowledge to know where to look for it and how to extract it.

The same is true of money: Knowledge is power, skills are power, and information is power, all of which can be transmuted into money when we know how.

What is interesting is that Knowledge, skills, and information are all perishable items. What do I mean by that?

Well, imagine you are living in the 18th century. Do you understand anything about flight or the internal combustion engine?

The Industrial Revolution was so named because the new Knowledge and understanding transformed millions of lives.

Today, Knowledge and understanding have continued to grow and flourish because skills and Knowledge are continuously refined. Even today, we must refine our skills, upgrade our knowledge, on an ongoing basis and then share it with others utilizing webinars and informational products with high perceived value.

Then, if you have a product or service with high perceived value, more people will want to buy it and be willing to pay a higher price to own it. If your skill set is that of a doctor or Lawyer, then the fees you can charge will be higher in perceived value than that of a refuse collector.

That's not to say refuse collectors have no value; that is not true. Without refuse collection, our cities would be overrun with pestilence in a matter of days.

There are thirty days of laws with my '30 days to change your mind, change your life' business' coaching program, full of important tips and information on changing your current reality into the reality you truly desire.

More details can be found at www.30daystochangeyour-mind.com.

Before we press on, let us recap what we have investigated so far.

In Chapter 1, we discussed Getting started on a new idea or project and how the brain works in a manner that can help or hinder us based on our previous life experiences. We discussed effectively setting goals, so our subconscious brain works with and not against us. Remember, the point is that whatever we put our thought energy into will become our current life experience.

Have you completed the exercises to set your goals? If not, please revisit chapter one and complete those critical tasks so that your mind is clear on how to shape your new reality to make it your new current reality. We then looked at buying your computer and what features you need to have on the computer to allow you to start using it as an effective business tool.

In Chapter 2, we discussed How pain can be used to identify how we can help both ourselves and reach people on an emotional level to help them solve their pain and problems. We looked at medical definitions of pain and psychological pain, which is the most imprisoning form of pain that keeps people stuck in a lifestyle they would sooner not have to endure. We looked at the monkey mind and how it chatters on and stops us from focusing on tasks we need to complete.

In Chapter 3, we discussed how to reach thousands of people within our chosen niche by understanding fundamentals such as the Know, Like, and Trust strategy. Before we ever contemplate selling any product or service. We learned that by showing empathy for our audience's pain and presenting them with working solutions, we can create a substantial following of hungry buyers for our product or service.

Affiliate marketing was highlighted to find products that have been proven to be successful, and YouTube, Facebook, and Google as platforms to present our adverts on.

In Chapter 4, we discussed the tools and services we need to set up to allow us to automate our business and the delivery of our products and services. In Chapter 5, we discussed: The types of resistance and hold-ups we will experience to some degree from family, friends, and other associates. We are encouraged to establish new friendships and business associates who will help and support our efforts to create our new business.

In Chapter 6, we have investigated our thinking patterns that are helping or hindering our progress thus far. This ongoing revelation must constantly be evaluated and corrected before we get to the financial security we need and aspire to attain. In the next chapter, we will discuss how to overcome failure and rejection, something that all internet marketers and millionaires experience daily.

CHAPTER 8

How to create adverts, what works and what does not work

Copywriting

Many copywriters start not with a computer but with a pen and small pieces of paper on which they write ideas, concepts, and headlines; they can spend hours and hours looking at phrase structure before ever a word is written on a computer.

Why do they do this, you may ask? Generally, it is because they are not alone in the room, and team members can spread out paper ideas on a desk, so the team can shortlist and discard ideas before returning to the keyboard to formulate shortlisted suggestions.

Copywriting is a crucial aspect of marketing and advertising; it requires a unique skill set to succeed. A copywriter creates compelling, engaging, and persuasive written content that sells products, services, or ideas. The role of a copywriter is to craft words that not only inform the reader but also invoke emotions and create an impression that lasts. You need to develop these essential skills to become a successful copywriter:

1. Excellent writing skills:

The most evident and fundamental skill a copywriter should possess is exceptional writing skills. A copywriter should have a firm grasp of grammar, punctuation, and sentence structure and be able to express ideas and thoughts clearly and concisely. They should also be able to write in various styles and tones, depending on the target audience and their content type.

2. Creativity:

Copywriting is not just about raising words on a page. Still, it's about creativity, imagination, and creating unique ideas and concepts. A copywriter should be able to think outside the box, write in a style that sets them apart from others, and craft compelling messages that capture the reader's attention.

3. Research:

Research is crucial in copywriting as it helps deeply understand the target audience and the industry. A copywriter should be able to conduct extensive research to gather information, find trends, and create data-driven content. This skill helps them to create content that is both relevant and persuasive to the target audience.

4. Strategic thinking:

Copywriting is not just about writing words but also about strategically writing them. A successful copywriter should know how to create adverts, what works and what does not work within an advert. Must be able to think critically and strategically and understand how to use words to achieve specific goals. They should be able to create a clear and concise message that speaks directly to the target audience and drives the desired action.

5. Attention to detail:

Attention to detail is critical in copywriting; a small mistake can significantly impact the results of an advertising campaign. A copywriter should be able to proofread their work thoroughly and ensure that their content is error-free and meets the required standards.

6. Adaptability:

The advertising and marketing industry is constantly evolving, and a successful copywriter should be able to adapt to the changes. They should be able to write in different styles, be open to new ideas, and learn and implement new techniques quickly.

7. Empathy:

Empathy is a crucial skill for copywriters as it helps them understand the target audience's needs and desires. Copywriters should be able to put themselves in the target audience's shoes and create content that resonates with them.

8.Marketing knowledge:

A copywriter should understand marketing principles, such as branding, consumer behavior, and marketing strategies. This knowledge helps him create content aligned with the company's marketing goals and objectives.

9. Collaboration:

Copywriting is not a solo task and often involves working with other team members such as designers, marketers, and developers. A successful copywriter should be able to collaborate effectively with others and work in a fast-paced and dynamic environment.

10. Digital skills:

In today's digital age, a copywriter should have a good understanding of digital media and be able to write content for various platforms such as websites, social media, e-mail, and mobile applications. They should be able to write engaging and compelling content optimized for the specific platform and audience. In conclusion, successful entrepreneurs require excellent writing skills, creativity, research, strategic thinking, attention to detail, and adaptability.

Advertising is an integral part of marketing, it reaches a large audience and drives awareness, interest, and action toward a product or service.

Creating effective advertisements requires understanding your target audience, knowing their pains, wants, and needs, and where to place your platform or channel where you will publish the advertisement.

Being creative with messaging and design is also the most important.

We will now discuss what works and does not work when creating adverts.

1. Know your target audience:

The first step in creating effective advertisements is understanding your target audience. You need to know who you are trying to reach and their needs, interests, and habits, and what is their most significant cause of pain?

Once the reader realizes that you are on their side and can relate to their pain, you create empathy with your target audience to create advertisements that resonate with them and drive their interest. You can gather this information through market research, customer surveys, and by analyzing your website data to see who is visiting and what they are interested in.

2. Know the platform and channel:

The next step is to understand the platform and channel where you will publish your advertisement. Each platform and channel have different strengths, weaknesses, and advertising formats.

For example, social media platforms like Facebook and Instagram have highly targeted advertising options. In contrast, search engines like Google have text-based advertisements.

Knowing the platform in the channel will help you create an optimized advertisement for that platform or channel.

3. Be creative with messaging and design:

The messaging undesigned of your advertisements is critical to their success. An advertisement should be eye-catching, memorable, and convey your message.

The messaging should be simple and concise, and the design should be aesthetically pleasing and consistent with your brand. You should also use high-quality images and graphics relevant to your product or service.

Ads that evoke an emotional response from the audience are often more effective than focusing solely on features and benefits.

Emotional appeal can come from telling a story, showcasing the impact of your product or service, or tapping into the desires and aspirations of your target audience.
Remember people buy on emotion most of the time.

4. Offer a call to action (CTA):

An advertisement should always include a clear call to action (CTA). A CTA is a message that encourages the audience to take specific action, such as visiting your website, purchasing, or signing up for a trial. The CTA should be clear, straightforward, and prominent in the advertisement.

5. Test and optimize.

Finally, it is essential to test and optimize your advertisements. Optimization means trying different variations of your advertisement and tracking the results to see what works best. You can use A/B testing to compare different ad versions and improve based on the results.

What Works:

1. Simple, clear messaging:

Adverts with simple, clear messaging tend to be more effective than cluttered and complex ones. Because people are more likely to remember and act on a simple message than one that is difficult to understand.

2. High-quality images and graphics:

Adverts that use high-quality images and graphics are more effective than low-quality or generic images. High-quality images and graphics can help make your advert more memorable and appealing.

3. Personalization:

Social and personalized to the target audience are more effective than those with our generic. Personalization can include using the target audience's name, location, or other information, such as how to create adverts, what works and what does not, and 93 personal information to make the ad more relevant and appealing.

4. Emotional appeal:

Adverts that evoke an emotional response from the audience tend to be more effective than those focused solely on features and benefits. Emotional appeal can come from telling a story that pulls on the audience's heartstrings or a story they can relate directly to.

Additional tips:

Let me ask you a question. What is the purpose of the headline in an advert?

Answer: The headline aims to grab the viewer's attention with clarity, indicating that they desire to read the sub-headline.

Let me ask you a second question
What is the purpose of the sub headline?

Answer: The purpose of the sub-headline is to keep the viewers' attention so that they desire to read the first line of the text.

A third question.
What is the purpose of the first line of the text?

Answer: The purpose of the first line of text is to engage the reader's attention so that they read the second line, ad infinitum.

This is how professional copywriters structure every successful advertisement.

Another aspect of every advert is that there must be a clear and precise call-to-action (CTA) such as a 'Click Here' sign, a 'Buy Now' sign, or a 'Learn More' sign.

Additionally, the color of the call-to-action button is significant.

The colour 'Red' generally means stop, so would you use a red button for the 'Buy Now' button?

Answer: Many marketers have spent thousands of dollars researching the optimum color and shade of color that encourages site visitors and advertisement readers to take the next step.

Pale green and light blue are all the preferred colors of most marketers who are successful in what they do.

In conclusion, copywriting and creating adverts is a skill and a craft. It behooves any entrepreneur or business owner to cultivate these skills for themselves, even if only to a level that allows them to effectively judge any advertisement before publication. By gaining this skillset, entrepreneurs quickly learn to recognize which advert style is more likely to succeed and which will crash and burn.

CHAPTER 9

My advert didn't work, what now? What to do when things don't go as expected

One thing we must understand from the outset when creating an advert is that:

"Nobody reads adverts, people read what interests them most. Sometimes, that is an advert."

– HOWARD GOSSAGE

Advertising is essential to any business's marketing strategy. However, sometimes an advertising campaign may generate a different result.

When this happens, assessing the situation and taking appropriate steps to improve the advert's performance is essential.

Here are some tips on what to do when an advert fails to produce the results you're seeking: The terminology for what we are about to do is called 'Split Testing.

1. Review the advert's performance:

The first step is to analyse the advert's performance metrics. We do this by checking how well the advert's engagement, clickthrough, and conversion rates performed to determine where the advert campaign needs to catch up. Gathering as much data as possible to identify the underlying issues is essential. Suppose you have used Facebook as a platform to advertise on, for example. In that case, they have an 'Ads Manager' section that breaks down everything to see where the ad is not meeting market expectations.

2. Identifying the problem:

Once you've identified the advert's performance, the next step is to identify if there are any other problems. Some common issues include poor targeting, weak messaging, and ineffective advert placement. For example, you would want to avoid selling cat food on a dog training website or trying to sell cosmetics to bodybuilders. Ensure your advert's niche, and your platform isn't full of other adverts irrelevant to your chosen niche. The more specific and accurate you can be in this regard will undoubtedly improve the audience participation in your advertising. Once you have identified which of these is the problem, you can work on developing a working solution, test it out with a small budget, and see what response you get.

3. Refining your advert:

Refining the advert is the next step in improving its performance. Based on your identified problem, you may need to just the messaging, and graphics, sometimes even changing the font and colours of the font in your advert to create an improved response. It is always wise to check and refine your target audience, or you can split the audience into male and female viewers to see who responds best. Make sure the advert is clear and concise, and visually appealing. Then test the new advert to see if the adjustments have improved its performance. Remember to test with a low daily budget and monitor the advert for performance. If the advert is performing worse than the original, switch it off so that you save your budget.

4. Change the advert's placement:

The advert's placement is critical to its success; consider changing your target to a different audience or placing it in a different format or platform. I'm referring to a different format if you have a lineage advert. For example, consider adding an image or a video to the text. Then, create a copy of the advert and place the copycat advert on a different platform. For example, if the text advert was on google, create a video advert with the exact text and place that on YouTube, Instagram, Tik Tok. Remember that each platform has different recommended lengths for the' reels' you post. (A Reel is a relatively new term for a short video). Alternatively, if the advert is not performing well on social media, consider placing it on a search engine.

5. Increase the advert's visibility:

We can increase the advert's visibility. In that case, we can improve its performance and consider increasing the advert's budget, but only when all the other metrics work well. By changing the advert's placement, we can ensure that it reaches a broader audience because our audience members have their preferences regarding the platform they commonly use. For example, advertising purely on TikTok will primarily exclude members of our audience who prefer Instagram or Facebook. Consider using multiple advert formats and platforms to increase the visibility of your advert.

6. Re-target the audience:

Re-targeting the audience is another very effective way to improve any adverts performance; this involves showing the advert to people who have already interacted with it or have visited your website. It is because it has now been well established in the business that your audience needs to see your advert at least seven times before they will interact with it.

Know, Like, and Trust are internet marketing elements essential to creating a relationship with prospective purchasers. Remember that most internet users are cautious about engaging with people they do not know. So many people in the world still have an image or vision in their mind that the Internet is full of scammers and rogues, yet, every day, they spend billions of dollars with Amazon and eBay, Etsy, and the like.

This hurdle is in the minds of the vast majority of internet users. The only way to overcome this false belief is by repeatedly exposing your product and services to members in your niche. A recognizable and memorable logo works so well once imprinted within the populace's minds as a product or service of value; they become lifelong customers.

Hopefully, now you are beginning to understand that the more targeted and specific your audience is, the more success we will have.

In conclusion, when an advert fails to produce results, we must analyze its performance and identify any underlying issues causing a lack of performance. When we refine our advert, we are looking to change its placement, increase its visibility, and then re-target the audience; these are all effective ways to improve the performance of any advert. By taking these steps, you can turn a failed advertising campaign into a successful one and achieve your marketing goals.

Let us dig a little deeper into this process.

When we refine our advert, we are looking to change its placement, increase its visibility, and then re-target the audience; these are all effective ways to improve the performance of any advert. By taking these steps, you can turn a failed advertising campaign into a successful one and achieve your marketing goals. Let us dig deeper into this process.

1. Define your target audience:

The first step is to define your target audience. First, identify your ideal customer's demographic, geographic, and psychographic characteristics.

By being this specific, you will tailor your advertising message in such a manner as to be accurate. determines the best channels to reach the people most likely to be interested in your product or service.

Demographic Characteristics are variables within a nation's population, such as age, gender, income level, marital status, ethnic origin, and education level; such demographic characteristics are a great way to segment each market you are targeting.

2. Use audience segmentation:

This is simply the Town, City, and Country where you are looking to place an advert.

You can even target your adverts to a specific postcode if you so desire.

Psychographic Characteristics include personality characteristics, lifestyle, social class, habits, behaviors, and interests.

Each of these unique psychological factors greatly influences a consumer's behavior; you then use these factors to segment your audience based on their psychographic makeup and, that way, monitor which segment responds best to which type of advert.

3. Use audience segmentation:

Segmenting your audience is a powerful way to target adverts. Suppose you divide your audience into smaller groups based on their interests, behavior, and demographics. By targeting smaller groups, you can create a more personalized message that resonates with each group more effectively.

For example, your target group is Golfers; you can subdivide that group into Age, Gender, Race, and even whether they are left-handed or right-handed golfers.

Once you start digging down your chosen niche, you will quickly see the most appropriate segments for your product or service.

4. Leverage social media:

Social media platforms are powerful tools for targeting adverts; most platforms offer granular targeting options based on interest behaviors and demographics. Also included are age, gender, and locations on the planet, even down to the local postcode.

These tools are so powerful that we can target 45-year-old males wearing green sweaters on a Tuesday. Well, it's not that intense, but you get my point.

Another feature of social media platforms is that they have kept a record of everybody who has viewed our interacted with your advert; this allows you the facility to re-target those specific people, thereby allowing you to present your adverts in front of people who have previously seen it thereby creating more of the know, like and trust scenario.

As mentioned earlier, the evidence suggests that people need to see your advert at least seven times before interacting with you in any positive manner.

5. Utilize search engine advertising:

Search engine advertising or SEO, which is search engine optimization, is the most effective way to target people actively seeking products, services, or solutions to a problem directly related to your business or service.

You can use keyword targeting to ensure your adverts appear in the relevant search results. Correctly using Keywords or, more accurately, Key Phrases allows for effective use of your budget by ensuring that only people interested in your product or service will see your adverts.

6. Take advantage of programmatic advertising:

Programmatic advertising is a form of automated advert buying that uses data to target specific audiences.

The Programmatic method allows you to reach people across multiple channels and devices simultaneously using real-time bidding, ensuring your adverts are displayed in front of the right people at the right time. This methodology is one that Agencies implement instead of using manual methods of advert placement.

Four major components comprise the basic framework of a programmatic advertising ecosystem.

a. Demand-side platform (DSP),
b. Supply-side platform (SSP),
c. Data management platform (DMP),
d. An advert exchange

Advert exchange is when each part of a given system works together to serve publishers and advertisers and allows them to trade effectively.

This method is a subject deserving a book all on its own. Advert exchange is a method used in business-to-business interactions, and I mention it only to inform you that the ways you can reach your audience are becoming more and more accurate and cost-effective.

7. Use location-based targeting:

Location-based targeting is a compelling way to reach people in specific geographic areas. This method benefits businesses with physical locations that wish to serve a specific region. It is mostly a technique that is used very effectively by advertising agencies.

If you were thinking of setting up your advertising agency, then you would use location-based targeting on social platforms to attract, for example, more customers to the local hairdresser or dog grooming salon when you require to have people physically visit a place of work.

8. Experiment with different advert formats:

Different advertising formats produce widely differing results with different audiences, so we need to experiment with different formats, such as video adverts, display adverts, and native adverts, to determine which works best for your target audience.

For example, younger audiences use TikTok mainly now. In contrast, with older audiences who still are on either Facebook or, in some instances, the older platform of Myspace.

To reach a certain type of person or character it is a good idea to create an 'avatar', which is the ideal way to establish a profile of the type of person we want to target for our product or service.

To do this we need to build a bio or an image, based on the characteristics of the type of person we wish to focus our advert on.

So, for example, if we target people coming up to retirement age who now realize that their pensions will no longer support them during their golden years, we would not be placing adverts on TikTok. We would focus on LinkedIn, Facebook groups, hard copy magazines on finance and investments, and newspapers with lineage adverts.

Recently, the old-fashioned method of creating lineage adverts in top-rated national newspapers with a link to a website is becoming quite effective, as it circumvents the noise of advertisements people see while browsing the Internet. One way of avoiding 'noise' is using native adverts.

Native adverts differ from standard adverts in fitting neatly inside the user's path through your site or app.

Visitors still know they are adverts but look great next to your content. Traditionally, they are known as advertorials

CHAPTER 10

The Difference Between a Mentor and a Coach

The terms' mentors' and 'coaches' are often used interchangeably, but they each bring unique qualities to the table. While both provide guidance, support, and advice, the nature of their relationship with the person they are helping to achieve the goals they are aiming for differs significantly.

A mentor, often an experienced and knowledgeable individual, serves as a role model and adviser to someone less experienced in their field. Beyond offering support, guidance, and feedback based on personal experiences and lessons learned, a mentor provides a crucial emotional support system. They help their mentees navigate challenges, set and achieve goals, and advise on methodologies that will develop skills and find new knowledge sources in their chosen field. The relationship between a mentor and a mentee can often extend over many years, supplying essential support and guidance, making the mentee feel understood and valued.

Coaches, on the other hand, are typically trained professionals who work with individuals or teams to help them achieve a specific goal or improve specific skills. Unlike mentors, coaches are not necessarily subject matter experts in their clients' fields. Instead, they use active listening, questioning, and goal-setting techniques to help clients identify and overcome obstacles, develop new skills, and achieve the desired goals. Meanwhile, coaches work with their clients to identify areas for improvement, set achievable and measurable goals, and develop a plan for reaching those goals. Coaching relationships are generally more focused and short-term, with a specific goal in mind.

Mentors and coaches, with their unique approaches, have the power to profoundly transform and elevate their clients' success and future development. Mentors, with their supportive and encouraging environment, help mentees cultivate self-confidence and a clear career direction. Coaches, on the other hand, assist clients in honing new skills, enhancing performance, and realizing their goals. Both mentors and coaches serve as a sounding board, aiding clients in navigating challenges and making crucial decisions, each offering a distinct perspective that is equally valuable.

Before we choose either a mentor or a coach, we must decide which will help us most effectively achieve our desired outcome. It would help if we considered several areas before selecting which profession will serve us best: a Mentor or a Coach. Here are a few guidelines to consider while making your decision.

What a Coach Can Do for Us?

1. Clarify our goals.

One of the first things the coach can help us do is clarify our goals. We often have a general idea of what we want to achieve but need a clear, specific, measurable plan. A coach can help us identify our strengths, weaknesses, and areas for improvement and work with us to develop a road map for achieving our goals. Creating a viable plan includes setting realistic timelines, breaking complex projects into more manageable tasks, and tracking progress.

2. Develop self-awareness

Self-awareness, a cornerstone of personal and professional growth, is a journey that a coach can guide us on. By posing thought-provoking questions, providing feedback and insights, and challenging our perspectives, a coach can help us gain a deeper understanding of our strengths, weaknesses, values, and beliefs. This self-awareness empowers us to make informed decisions, communicate effectively, and foster stronger relationships, thereby boosting our self-assurance and personal growth.

3. Build confidence

Having an outward appearance of confidence is essential for success in any area of life. A coach can help us build confidence by encouraging, supporting, and validating that our efforts and achievements will stop. They can also help you identify areas where we may be holding ourselves back and work with us to develop strategies for overcoming self-doubt and fear. By eliminating self-doubt and fear, our confidence in ourselves will increase, and we can take on new challenges, pursue our passions, and achieve our goals more quickly.

4. Improve communication skills.

Effective communication is a critical skill for success in any field. A coach can help you improve your communication skills by providing verbal and non-view double-communication feedback. By nonverbal communication, we're talking about posture, poise, and body language, which provide as much as 80% of communication between human beings. Many public speakers use body language to get their point across to a large audience effectively; by adapting and using those skills, you can more effectively communicate your thoughts, ideas, and desired outcomes to your audience, be they an individual, a board of directors, or a receptive audience. By improving your communication skills, you can build stronger relationships, resolve conflicts more effectively, and succeed tremendously in your personal and professional endeavors.

5. Increase accountability

Being held accountable is essential for achieving your goals, as it is easy to self-deceive and believe you're making progress when all you are doing is procrastinating. The mentor or a coach will help you increase accountability by holding you to your commitments. These are the plans and timelines that you discussed previously. Through regular contact, they will ensure you stay on track. By following this planned strategy, you will overcome obstacles with your coach or mentor's help, support, and encouragement. Helping you keep motivated and focused on your goals, even when challenges and setbacks can sometimes make you feel like packing it all in.

6. Enhanced problem-solving skills

Problem-solving is an essential skill for success in any field. A coach can help us develop our problem-solving skills by helping us identify and define problems, brainstorm solutions, and evaluate the effectiveness of different proteins. Very often, when one is in the center of an event, it can be challenging, and sometimes, one is blinded by solutions only identified by an outside person with a critical understanding of the situation. When we have developed more vital problem-solving skills, we will be more effective at resolving conflicts between staff members or suppliers, making decisions in general, and achieving our goals.

7. Develop leadership skills.

Leadership skills are essential for success in business, education, healthcare, and many other fields. A coach can help us develop leadership skills by guiding effective communication, strategic thinking, conflict resolution, and team building. By developing strong leadership skills, we will become a more effective and influential leader in our organization or community.

8. Improve time management skills.

Time management skills must be stressed more highly, as they are essential for achieving goals and maintaining a healthy work-life balance. A coach can help you improve your time management skills by helping you prioritize tasks, develop a schedule that works best for you, and eliminate time-wasting activities. With improved time management skills, we can achieve more in less time and reduce stress and burnout.

One critical element is considering what we do daily and evaluating whether the time we spend on a given task produces income, drains income, improves health, or weakens health. Doing domestic chores such as washing, ironing, cooking, cleaning, etc., can be far better managed by employing a person to do the things you would typically spend many hours doing.

Employing a domestic helper will free up time for you to earn a higher income level instead of utilizing your rate to undertake menial but necessary tasks. But, if we value our time at $100 an hour and the time that we would pay a cleaner is $20 an hour, it makes sense to employ a person to do menial tasks for a fair labor rate than it does for us, whose labor value is $100/hour or more

What a Mentor Can Do for Us?

1. Offer guidance and support.

One of the main benefits of having a mentor is that they can offer guidance if you are struggling. A mentor can help you navigate challenging situations, offer advice on handling difficult people or scenarios, and provide insights on overcoming obstacles. Having someone who has been through similar situations and can offer a different perspective can be invaluable in helping you achieve your goals.

2. Share knowledge and expertise.

Another benefit of having a mentor is that they can share their knowledge and expertise with us. Mentors are usually highly skilled and experienced in their field. They can often offer insights and advice on subjects considered to be trade secrets, which can help us grow and develop in our careers or personal lives. Whether it's sharing specific techniques or processes, offering success tips, or providing access to their network of contacts, having a mentor can give us a significant advantage over our competitors.

3. Provide networking opportunities.

Mentors often have extensive contacts within their industry or field, and they could present or suggest valuable networking opportunities to you. Introducing you to people who can help you advance your career, provide new opportunities, or offer advice and support can be valuable. Mentors can help us secure job interviews or recommend new positions in places we may need to be aware of.

4. Offer feedback and advice.

Another benefit of having a Mentor is that they can offer us feedback and advice on our work or progress. Whether it's providing critiques of our performance or offering suggestions on how to improve, having someone who can offer objective feedback can be invaluable in helping us grow and develop. Mentors can also offer advice on handling difficult situations or navigating tricky scenarios, providing us with the tools we need to ensure that we succeed.

5. Challenge you to grow.

Mentors can also challenge you to grow and develop in ways you may not have thought possible. By pushing you out of your comfort zone, mentors can help you take on new challenges, learn new skills, and overcome obstacles you may have thought were insurmountable. Once overcome, you become a stronger, more capable person. You can help you to achieve your goals more quickly and effectively.

6. Provide emotional support.

Starting in business or engaging in a scenario outside your comfort zone can become highly emotional. Having a mentor who has previously experienced the same or similar scenario can guide you through the ups and downs of having your own business. Mentors have an invested interest in your success and well-being, and they can and will offer a listening ear and a shoulder to lean on when you need it the most. Whether you're dealing with a difficult personal situation or struggling to overcome a professional setback or set of circumstances, having someone who cares about you and your success, who is also willing and capable of supporting you perfectly, will make all the difference to the outcome.

7. Encourage self-reflection.

Mentors also encourage us to have self-reflection, which is an essential component of personal and professional growth. We are often so wound up in the environment that we fail to realize how far we have traveled.

Please take a moment to look back and evaluate where we started; seeing past challenges defeated and obstacles overcome can be a most welcome boost to the soul.

Your mentor may ask you thought-provoking questions and challenge you to think deeply about your goals and aspirations; mentors can help you better understand yourself and what you want out of life.

Once you are specifically aware of what you want out of life, you become very specific in making informed decisions, communicating more effectively, building stronger relationships, and having a better quality of life for you and your family.

8. Help you build self-confidence.

Finally, having a Mentor can help us build confidence; by providing guidance, support, and encouragement, Mentors can help us believe in ourselves and our abilities.

Having someone in our circle of trusted advisors, like a Mentor, who has already walked the path we are walking creates a significant confidence boost. Knowing that there's somebody you can speak to on a telephone, Skype call, or Zoom meeting who is on the same wavelength as us and who has already experienced obstacles and pitfalls is especially important when we are starting on our new career path.

It is especially true when and if we are facing significant challenges or obstacles.

Having a mentor or multiple mentors has often been the critical element in helping the world's captains of industry and commerce, as we see daily in the public arena.

Now it's ALL about You.

I'm sure you've heard the expression many times before: 'At the end of the day, whether you achieve the success you desire is entirely in your own hands.' While it is probably true when one considers a person dedicated to success undertakes the work and the ethics involved to drive their ambition to a successful outcome. However, there is an enemy in your camp; this enemy doesn't deem itself to be the enemy; no, this entity, this ego, this little voice in your head, howsoever you describe it, is only interested in preserving your well-being based on previous life experiences environment of childhood and indeed the peers that surround you in your daily life.

Some more advanced coaches and mentors regard this entity as the 'Gatekeeper of our mind.' As we've mentioned elsewhere in this book, our subconscious and super-conscious minds work each from their standpoint based on our previous life experiences. Each has a goal to keep us safe and maintain the Status Quo.

These two gatekeepers will either permit us to succeed or de-rail us and cause us to fail in our endeavors. We each have a built-in 'thermostat,' so to speak, which is, in fact, our subconscious mind, which, unbeknown to most of us, controls what our mind regards as to what is viable or realistic for us to achieve.

You cannot lie to yourself.

One could liken this to the analogy of the Flea in the Jar. If you have not heard of that analogy, A Flea can jump up to approximately 12 feet or 4 meters. However, if you place the Flea in a jar with a lid on, every time it tries to jump, it bangs into the lid of the Jar. So, the Flea learns not to jump higher than the height of the Jar. If you then, after a time, we release the Flea from the Jar, it will only jump two or three inches (75mm).

Why?

The circumstances imposed on its life have restricted its mental capacity to a level that it does not believe it can jump the distance other fleas can. Crudely, what happens to us when we experience certain events makes us think we cannot do this or that when, in fact, we are each more than capable of doing anything we desire within the bounds of human abilities.

If we venture out of the preset range, self-sabotage sets in, and we can find ourselves back where we started or worse. Because of this, we need to engage in Strategic planning to ensure that both our gatekeepers (the conscious and sub-conscious minds) are working with us on this new endeavor. We can create a strategy that works in principle in the business world. However, you can still experience disappointments, setbacks, or other intrusions into our brilliant plans if our gatekeepers are off our side. Meditation, with practice, becomes a powerful tool for communicating with our inner being.

For all your designs, plans, and ambitions to succeed, you must get your inner gatekeeper working in harmony with those plans and desires. Accessing the gatekeeper of the mind can be achieved by several methods, such as self-hypnosis, neuro-linguistic programming (NLP), meditation, the use of mind movies, and listening to music played to a tuning of 526 Hertz implementing binaural beats. You can research these strategies thoroughly on both Google and YouTube, and I encourage you to search out and experiment with these methodologies.

There's a significant amount of information available on each of these topics, far more than can be covered within the scope of this book. However, in my coaching and mentoring programs, I delve into each of these subjects in detail; as an aid to help you get started, I have included a link to my '30 Days to Change Your Mind, Change Your Destiny' program, which is an introduction to some of these techniques.

In closing, do not strive for perfection but ensure your daily goal is to get something done every day that progresses you to your desired goal or outcome. Expect challenges daily, setbacks frequently, and disappointments occasionally, but no matter what you encounter on your journey to your new life, never give up. Each day is a new opportunity to forge onward and upward; you only fail when you stop doing.

Do not fear mistakes; there is no failure, only lessons to learn and new skills to conquer. And remember to enjoy your journey as it never ends; there are no destinations in life, only marker posts of your achievements.

Made in the USA
Monee, IL
04 November 2026

67388658R10066